Forms at Your Fingertips

W9-BZX-416

Table of Contents

From the desk of Ms. Lightcap

About This Book

Inside this all-new compilation—*Forms at Your Fingertips*—you'll find over 150 handy forms to help you manage your classroom, plan instruction, and communicate with both students and parents. Designed in seasonal and open formats, you'll find forms such as lists and labels, notes and organizers, and posters and planning sheets that you can use time and time again throughout the entire year! *Forms at Your Fingertips* is one resource you can't be without!

Managing Editor: Elizabeth H. Lindsay
Editor at Large: Diane Badden
Copy Editors: Tazmen Carlisle, Amy Kirtley-Hill, Kristy Parton, Debbie Shoffner, Cathy Edwards Simrell
Cover Artist: Clevell Harris
Art Coordinators: Theresa Lewis Goode, Stuart Smith
Artists: Pam Crane, Chris Curry, Shane Freeman, Theresa Lewis Goode, Clevell Harris, Ivy L. Koonce, Clint Moore, Greg D. Rieves, Rebecca Saunders, Barry Slate, Stuart Smith, Donna K. Teal
The Mailbox® Books.com: Judy P. Wyndham (MANAGER); Jennifer Tipton Bennett (DESIGNER/ARTIST); Karen White (INTERNET COORDINATOR); Paul Fleetwood, Xiaoyun Wu (SYSTEMS)

President, The Mailbox Book Company®: Joseph C. Bucci
Director of Book Planning and Development: Chris Poindexter
Curriculum Director: Karen P. Shelton
Book Development Managers: Cayce Guiliano, Elizabeth H. Lindsay, Thad McLaurin
Editorial Planning: Kimberley Bruck (DIRECTOR); Debra Liverman, Sharon Murphy, Susan Walker (TEAM LEADERS)
Editorial and Freelance Management: Karen A. Brudnak; Sarah Hamblet, Hope Rodgers (EDITORIAL ASSISTANTS)
Editorial Production: Lisa K. Pitts (TRAFFIC MANAGER); Lynette Dickerson (TYPE SYSTEMS); Mark Rainey (TYPESETTER)
Librarian: Dorothy C. McKinney

www.themailbox.com

©2004 by THE EDUCATION CENTER, INC.
All rights reserved.
ISBN10 #1-56234-584-2 • ISBN13 #978-156234-584-6

Except as provided for herein, no part of this publication may be reproduced or transmitted in any form or by any means, electronic or mechanical, including photocopying, recording, or storing in any information storage and retrieval system or electronic online bulletin board, without prior written permission from The Education Center, Inc. Permission is given to the original purchaser to reproduce patterns and reproducibles for individual classroom use only and not for resale or distribution. Reproduction for an entire school or school system is prohibited. Please direct written inquiries to The Education Center, Inc., P.O. Box 9753, Greensboro, NC 27429-0753. The Education Center®, The Mailbox®, the mailbox/post/grass logo, and The Mailbox Book Company® are registered trademarks of The Education Center, Inc. All other brand or product names are trademarks or registered trademarks of their respective companies.

Manufactured in the United States
10 9 8 7 6 5 4

Classroom Management

Classroom Management

Classroom Management

Classroom Management

Classroom Management

Classroom Management

Class List: Fall

1.
2.
3.
4.
5.

SPECIAL CLASS SCH

Class		Monday	Tuesday	Wednesday
MUSIC	Time:			
P.E.	Time:			
LIBRARY	Time:			

teacher

Behavior

Our Class Rules!

School & Classroom

REWARDS!

AUGUST

Sunday	Monday	Tuesday	Wednesday	Thursday	Friday	Saturday

©The Education Center, Inc. • Forms at Your Fingertips • TEC60824

September

Sunday	Monday	Tuesday	Wednesday	Thursday	Friday	Saturday

©The Education Center, Inc. • Forms at Your Fingertips • TEC60824

October

Sunday	Monday	Tuesday	Wednesday	Thursday	Friday	Saturday

©The Education Center, Inc. • Forms at Your Fingertips • TEC60824

November

Sunday	Monday	Tuesday	Wednesday	Thursday	Friday	Saturday

©The Education Center, Inc. • Forms at Your Fingertips • TEC60824

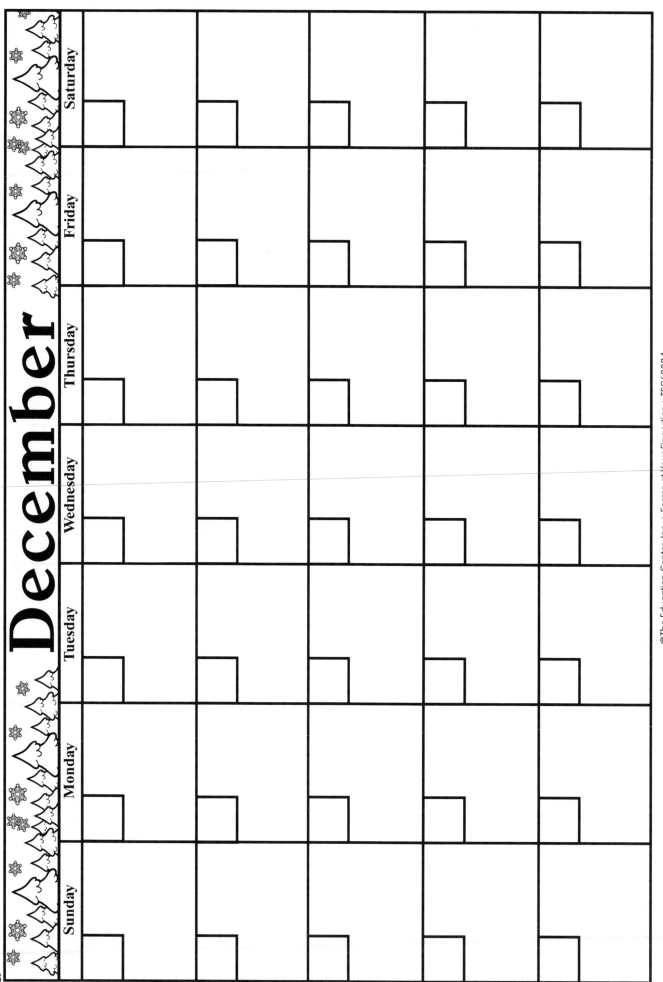

December

Sunday	Monday	Tuesday	Wednesday	Thursday	Friday	Saturday

©The Education Center, Inc. • Forms at Your Fingertips • TEC60824

JANUARY

Sunday	Monday	Tuesday	Wednesday	Thursday	Friday	Saturday

©The Education Center, Inc. • Forms at Your Fingertips • TEC60824

February

Sunday	Monday	Tuesday	Wednesday	Thursday	Friday	Saturday

©The Education Center, Inc. • Forms at Your Fingertips • TEC60824

March

Sunday	Monday	Tuesday	Wednesday	Thursday	Friday	Saturday

©The Education Center, Inc. • Forms at Your Fingertips • TEC60824

APRIL

Sunday	Monday	Tuesday	Wednesday	Thursday	Friday	Saturday

©The Education Center, Inc. • Forms at Your Fingertips • TEC60824

MAY

Sunday	Monday	Tuesday	Wednesday	Thursday	Friday	Saturday

©The Education Center, Inc. • Forms at Your Fingertips • TEC60824

JUNE

Sunday	Monday	Tuesday	Wednesday	Thursday	Friday	Saturday

©The Education Center, Inc. • Forms at Your Fingertips • TEC60824

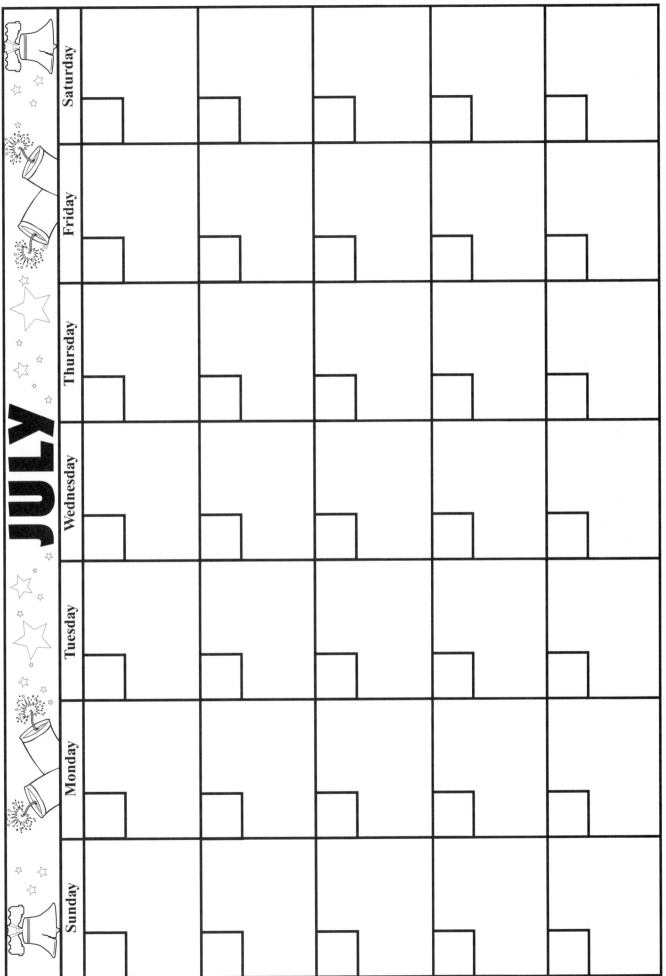

JULY

Sunday	Monday	Tuesday	Wednesday	Thursday	Friday	Saturday

©The Education Center, Inc. • Forms at Your Fingertips • TEC60824

Student Information Card

First name _____ Last name _____

Address _____

City _____ State _____ Zip _____

Mother's name _____ Mother's phone _____

Father's name _____ Father's phone _____

Student no.

Student's birthdate _____

Mother's email _____

Father's email _____

Comments: _____
_____

Medical concerns: _____
_____

Emergency contact _____

Emergency phone _____

Transportation to and from school: _____ walks _____ rides bus (#_____) _____ other

©The Education Center, Inc. • Forms at Your Fingertips • TEC60824

Student Information Card

First name _____ Last name _____

Address _____

City _____ State _____ Zip _____

Mother's name _____ Mother's phone _____

Father's name _____ Father's phone _____

Student no.

Student's birthdate _____

Mother's email _____

Father's email _____

Comments: _____
_____

Medical concerns: _____
_____

Emergency contact _____

Emergency phone _____

Transportation to and from school: _____ walks _____ rides bus (#_____) _____ other

©The Education Center, Inc. • Forms at Your Fingertips • TEC60824

Class Information

	Name	Birthday	Parent Name	Home No.	Work No.
1.					
2.					
3.					
4.					
5.					
6.					
7.					
8.					
9.					
10.					
11.					
12.					
13.					
14.					
15.					
16.					
17.					
18.					
19.					
20.					
21.					
22.					
23.					
24.					
25.					
26.					
27.					
28.					
29.					
30.					

Transportation List

Teacher: _____
Room No.: _____
Grade: _____

Bus Riders   **Bus #**

Other

Walkers

Car Riders

©The Education Center, Inc. • Forms at Your Fingertips • TEC60824

1.												
2.												
3.												
4.												
5.												
6.												
7.												
8.												
9.												
10.												
11.												
12.												
13.												
14.												
15.												
16.												
17.												
18.												
19.												
20.												
21.												
22.												
23.												
24.												
25.												
26.												
27.												
28.												
29.												
30.												

Class List: Fall

1.												
2.												
3.												
4.												
5.												
6.												
7.												
8.												
9.												
10.												
11.												
12.												
13.												
14.												
15.												
16.												
17.												
18.												
19.												
20.												
21.												
22.												
23.												
24.												
25.												
26.												
27.												
28.												
29.												
30.												

©The Education Center, Inc. • *Forms at Your Fingertips* • TEC60824

1.												
2.												
3.												
4.												
5.												
6.												
7.												
8.												
9.												
10.												
11.												
12.												
13.												
14.												
15.												
16.												
17.												
18.												
19.												
20.												
21.												
22.												
23.												
24.												
25.												
26.												
27.												
28.												
29.												
30.												

Class List: Spring

1.												
2.												
3.												
4.												
5.												
6.												
7.												
8.												
9.												
10.												
11.												
12.												
13.												
14.												
15.												
16.												
17.												
18.												
19.												
20.												
21.												
22.												
23.												
24.												
25.												
26.												
27.												
28.												
29.												
30.												

©The Education Center, Inc. • *Forms at Your Fingertips* • TEC60824

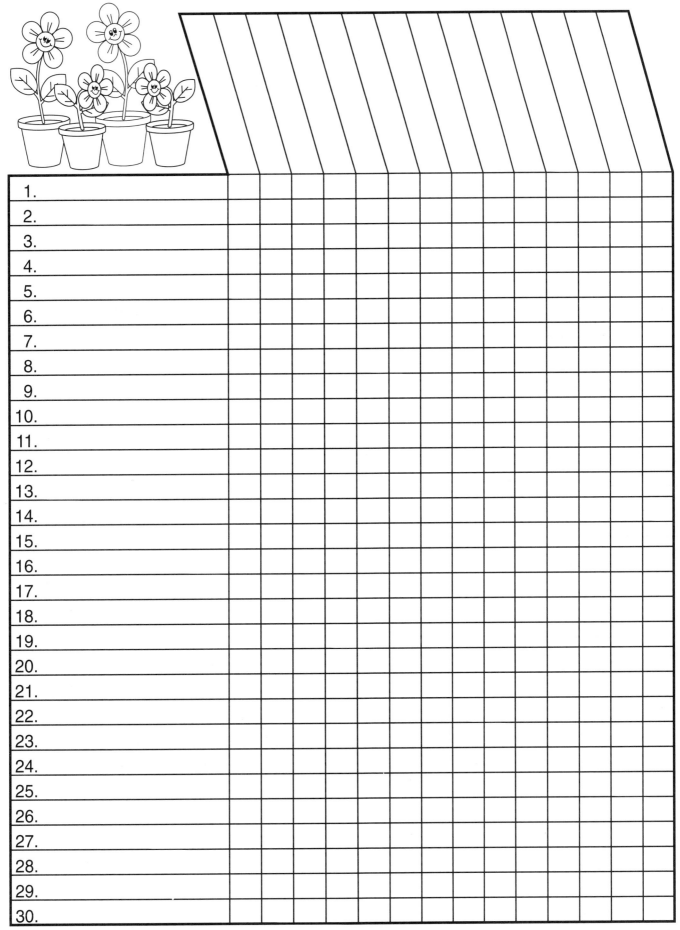

1.										
2.										
3.										
4.										
5.										
6.										
7.										
8.										
9.										
10.										
11.										
12.										
13.										
14.										
15.										
16.										
17.										
18.										
19.										
20.										
21.										
22.										
23.										
24.										
25.										
26.										
27.										
28.										
29.										
30.										

Weekly Activity Schedule

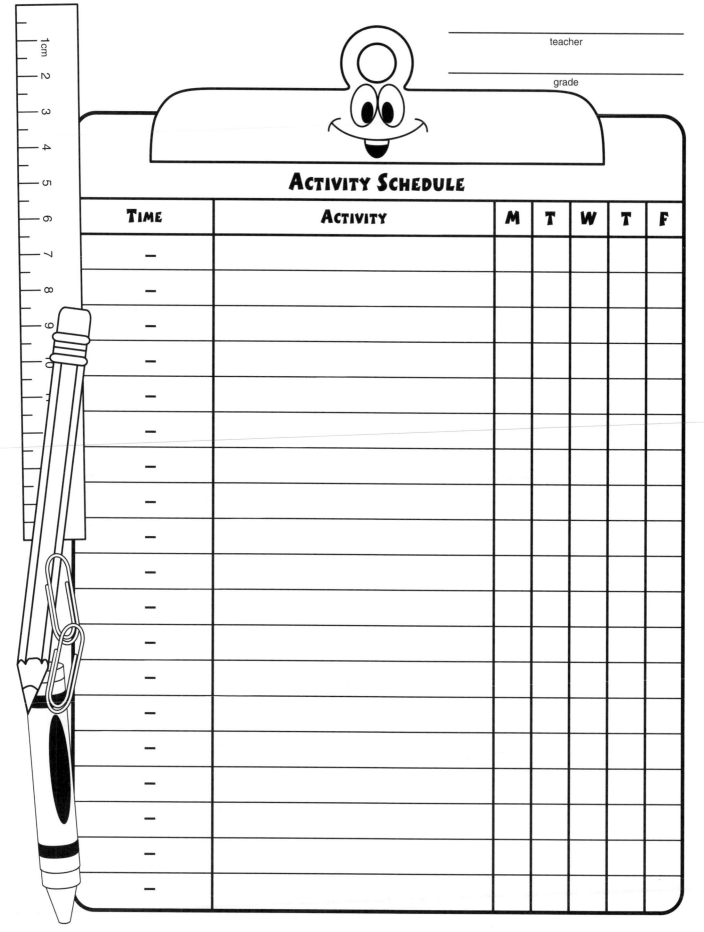

teacher _____

grade _____

ACTIVITY SCHEDULE

TIME	ACTIVITY	M	T	W	T	F
–						
–						
–						
–						
–						
–						
–						
–						
–						
–						
–						
–						
–						
–						
–						
–						
–						
–						

©The Education Center, Inc. • Forms at Your Fingertips • TEC60824

SPECIAL CLASS SCHEDULE

teacher _____   grade _____

Class	Monday	Tuesday	Wednesday	Thursday	Friday
MUSIC Time:					
P.E. Time:					
LIBRARY Time:					
ART Time:					
COMPUTER Time:					
Time:					

Students attending other classes (speech, band, etc.): _____

©The Education Center, Inc. • Forms at Your Fingertips • TEC60824

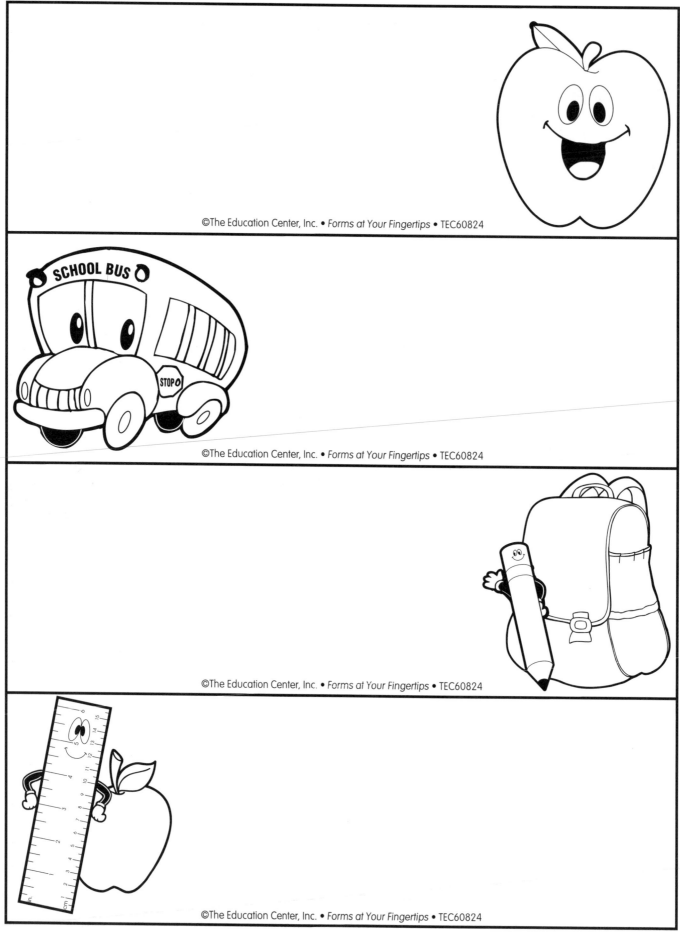

©The Education Center, Inc. • *Forms at Your Fingertips* • TEC60824

©The Education Center, Inc. • *Forms at Your Fingertips* • TEC60824

©The Education Center, Inc. • *Forms at Your Fingertips* • TEC60824

©The Education Center, Inc. • *Forms at Your Fingertips* • TEC60824

Hall Pass

_____
teacher

©The Education Center, Inc. • *Forms at Your Fingertips* • TEC60824

Rest Room Pass

_____
teacher

©The Education Center, Inc. • *Forms at Your Fingertips* • TEC60824

Office Pass

OFFICE PASS

_____
teacher

©The Education Center, Inc. • *Forms at Your Fingertips* • TEC60824

Library Pass

_____
teacher

©The Education Center, Inc. • *Forms at Your Fingertips* • TEC60824

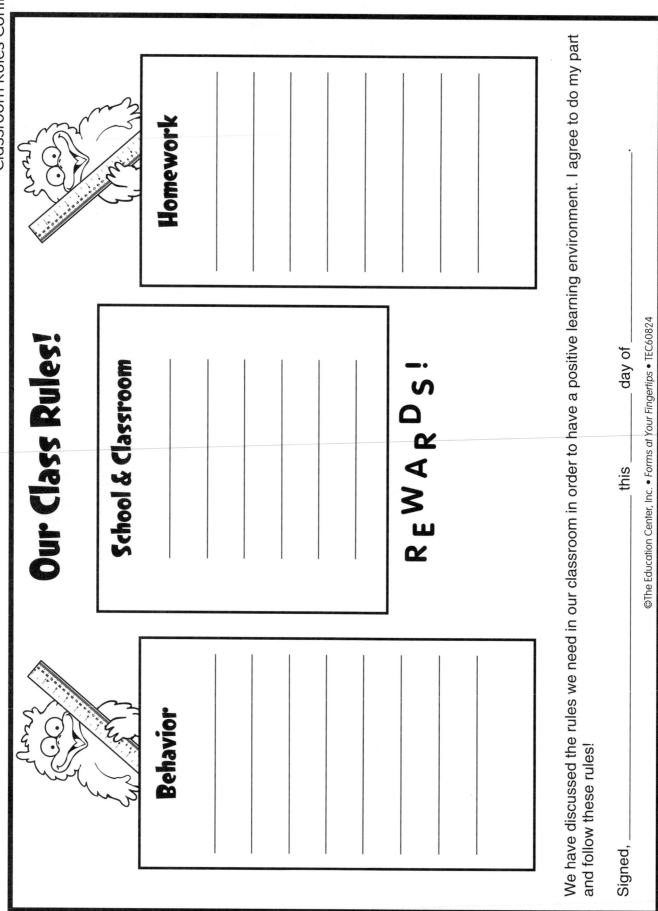

Our Class Rules!

Homework

School & Classroom

Behavior

RE W A R D s!

We have discussed the rules we need in our classroom in order to have a positive learning environment. I agree to do my part and follow these rules!

Signed, _____ this _____ day of _____ .

©The Education Center, Inc. • Forms at Your Fingertips • TEC60824

Homework Policy

Dear Parent,

Homework is an important part of your child's school experience. Supporting good work habits requires a joint effort. I will support your child and encourage good work habits at school. Your child will benefit greatly from your support and encouragement at home.

Please read the homework policy below and discuss it with your child. **Then sign the lower portion of this form and return it to school with your child.** Be sure to keep this portion of the form for future reference.

Homework Policy

_____

_____

_____

_____

_____

Rewards: _____

_____

_____

Sincerely,

_____
teacher

_____
date

©The Education Center, Inc. • *Forms at Your Fingertips* • TEC60824

I have read the homework policy. I have also discussed the policy with my child.

_____
parent signature

_____
student name

_____
date

WEEKLY HOMEWORK ASSIGNMENT SHEET

Monday _____
date

Tuesday _____
date

Wednesday _____
date

Thursday _____
date

Friday _____
date

©The Education Center, Inc. • *Forms at Your Fingertips* • TEC60824

Good Work Coupon
Redeem this coupon for

_____

_____

_____

(student name)

©The Education Center, Inc. • *Forms at Your Fingertips* • TEC60824

Good Work Coupon
Redeem this coupon for

_____

_____

_____

(student name)

©The Education Center, Inc. • *Forms at Your Fingertips* • TEC60824

Good Work Coupon
Redeem this coupon for

_____

_____

_____

(student name)

©The Education Center, Inc. • *Forms at Your Fingertips* • TEC60824

Good Work Coupon
Redeem this coupon for

_____

_____

_____

(student name)

©The Education Center, Inc. • *Forms at Your Fingertips* • TEC60824

Good Work Coupon
Redeem this coupon for

_____

_____

_____

(student name)

©The Education Center, Inc. • *Forms at Your Fingertips* • TEC60824

Good Work Coupon
Redeem this coupon for

_____

_____

_____

(student name)

©The Education Center, Inc. • *Forms at Your Fingertips* • TEC60824

Good Work Coupon
Redeem this coupon for

_____

_____

_____

(student name)

©The Education Center, Inc. • *Forms at Your Fingertips* • TEC60824

Good Work Coupon
Redeem this coupon for

_____

_____

_____

(student name)

©The Education Center, Inc. • *Forms at Your Fingertips* • TEC60824

Behavior and Discipline Policies

Dear Parent,

   Your child's success is very important. To create and maintain a positive learning environment for all students, I will follow the behavior and discipline policies below. Please read them and discuss them with your child. **Then sign the lower portion of this form and return it to school with your child.** Be sure to keep this portion of the form for future reference.

Behavior Policy

_____

_____

_____

_____

Rewards for good behavior: _____

_____

Discipline Policy

_____

_____

_____

_____

Sincerely,

_____
teacher

_____
date

- -

I have read the behavior and discipline policies. I have also discussed these policies with my child.

_____   _____
parent signature   student name

_____
date

©The Education Center, Inc. • *Forms at Your Fingertips* • TEC60824

Behavior Documentation

Grade: _____ Room No.: _____

Teacher: _____

Dates: _____

Student Name	Behavior	Date	Action Taken	Parent Contact/Response

Communication Log

Contacts with _____
parent name

_____
child's name

Date: _____ Time: _____ Method of contact: ☐ phone ☐ in person ☐ email ☐ _____	Reason for contact:	Notes:
Date: _____ Time: _____ Method of contact: ☐ phone ☐ in person ☐ email ☐ _____	Reason for contact:	Notes:
Date: _____ Time: _____ Method of contact: ☐ phone ☐ in person ☐ email ☐ _____	Reason for contact:	Notes:
Date: _____ Time: _____ Method of contact: ☐ phone ☐ in person ☐ email ☐ _____	Reason for contact:	Notes:

©The Education Center, Inc. • Forms at Your Fingertips • TEC60824

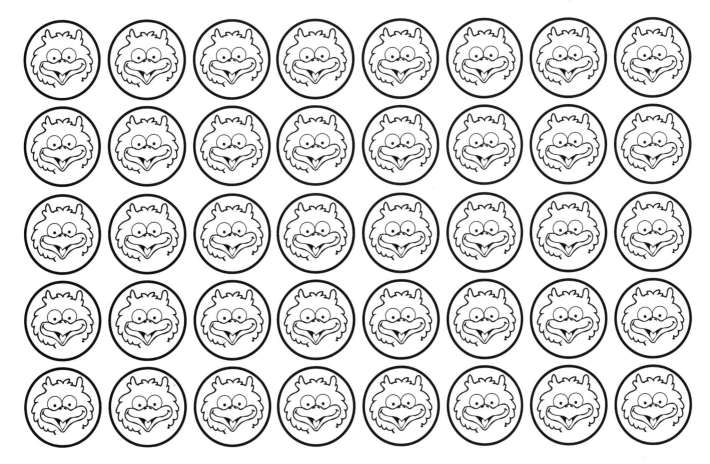

Good Behavior Coupon
Redeem this coupon for

_____

_____

_____

_____
(student name)

©The Education Center, Inc. • *Forms at Your Fingertips* • TEC60824

Good Behavior Coupon
Redeem this coupon for

_____

_____

_____

_____
(student name)

©The Education Center, Inc. • *Forms at Your Fingertips* • TEC60824

Good Behavior Coupon
Redeem this coupon for

_____

_____

_____

_____
(student name)

©The Education Center, Inc. • *Forms at Your Fingertips* • TEC60824

Good Behavior Coupon
Redeem this coupon for

_____

_____

_____

_____
(student name)

©The Education Center, Inc. • *Forms at Your Fingertips* • TEC60824

Name _____ Incentive chart

©The Education Center, Inc. • *Forms at Your Fingertips* • TEC60824

Name _____ Incentive chart

©The Education Center, Inc. • *Forms at Your Fingertips* • TEC60824

Name _____ Incentive chart

©The Education Center, Inc. • *Forms at Your Fingertips* • TEC60824

Name _____ Incentive chart

©The Education Center, Inc. • *Forms at Your Fingertips* • TEC60824

Name _____ Incentive chart

©The Education Center, Inc. • *Forms at Your Fingertips* • TEC60824

Name _____ Incentive chart

©The Education Center, Inc. • *Forms at Your Fingertips* • TEC60824

Name _____ Incentive chart

©The Education Center, Inc. • *Forms at Your Fingertips* • TEC60824

Name _____ Incentive chart

©The Education Center, Inc. • *Forms at Your Fingertips* • TEC60824

Name _____ Incentive chart

©The Education Center, Inc. • *Forms at Your Fingertips* • TEC60824

Name _____ Incentive chart

©The Education Center, Inc. • *Forms at Your Fingertips* • TEC60824

Name _____ Incentive chart

©The Education Center, Inc. • *Forms at Your Fingertips* • TEC60824

Name _____ Incentive chart

©The Education Center, Inc. • *Forms at Your Fingertips* • TEC60824

Introducing _____

name

Complete the sentence starters.

1. My favorite subjects are _____

_____

2. My hobbies are _____

_____

3. After school I _____

_____

4. I wish I could _____

_____

5. I would like to meet _____

_____

6. Sometimes I am _____

7. When I am older _____

_____

8. My family is _____

_____

9. I would like to visit _____

_____

10. The most important thing to me is _____

_____

11. I am happy when _____

_____

12. I do not like _____

_____

13. A great thing about me is _____

_____

©The Education Center, Inc. • Forms at Your Fingertips • TEC60824

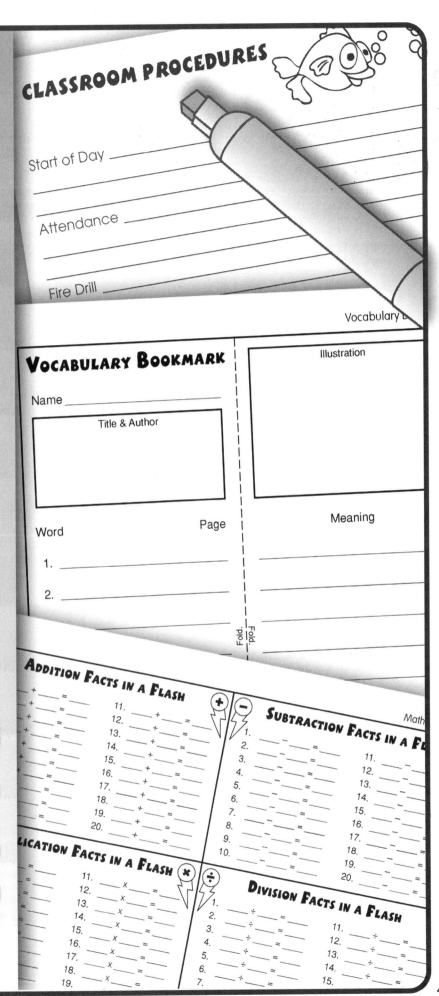

CLASSROOM PROCEDURES

Start of Day _____

Attendance _____

Fire Drill _____

Vocabulary

VOCABULARY BOOKMARK

Name _____

Title & Author

Illustration

Word   Page

1. _____

2. _____

Meaning

Fold.

ADDITION FACTS IN A FLASH

___ + ___ = ___
___ + ___ = ___
___ + ___ = ___
___ + ___ = ___
___ + ___ = ___
___ + ___ = ___

11. ___ + ___ = ___
12. ___ + ___ = ___
13. ___ + ___ = ___
14. ___ + ___ = ___
15. ___ + ___ = ___
16. ___ + ___ = ___
17. ___ + ___ = ___
18. ___ + ___ = ___
19. ___ + ___ = ___
20. ___ + ___ = ___

SUBTRACTION FACTS IN A FLASH

1. ___ − ___ = ___
2. ___ − ___ = ___
3. ___ − ___ = ___
4. ___ − ___ = ___
5. ___ − ___ = ___
6. ___ − ___ = ___
7. ___ − ___ = ___
8. ___ − ___ = ___
9. ___ − ___ = ___
10. ___ − ___ = ___

11. ___ − ___ = ___
12. ___ − ___ = ___
13. ___ − ___ = ___
14. ___ − ___ = ___
15. ___ − ___ = ___
16. ___ − ___ = ___
17. ___ − ___ = ___
18. ___ − ___ = ___
19. ___ − ___ = ___
20. ___ − ___ = ___

MULTIPLICATION FACTS IN A FLASH

11. ___ × ___ = ___
12. ___ × ___ = ___
13. ___ × ___ = ___
14. ___ × ___ = ___
15. ___ × ___ = ___
16. ___ × ___ = ___
17. ___ × ___ = ___
18. ___ × ___ = ___
19. ___ × ___ = ___

DIVISION FACTS IN A FLASH

1. ___ ÷ ___ = ___
2. ___ ÷ ___ = ___
3. ___ ÷ ___ = ___
4. ___ ÷ ___ = ___
5. ___ ÷ ___ = ___
6. ___ ÷ ___ = ___
7. ___ ÷ ___ = ___

11. ___ ÷ ___ = ___
12. ___ ÷ ___ = ___
13. ___ ÷ ___ = ___
14. ___ ÷ ___ = ___
15. ___ ÷ ___ = ___

Yearly Planning Calendar

August	September	October	November	December	January

©The Education Center, Inc. • Forms at Your Fingertips • TEC60824

Yearly Planning Calendar

February	March	April	May	June	July

©The Education Center, Inc. • Forms at Your Fingertips • TEC60824

Monthly Planning Form

Month: _____

©The Education Center, Inc. • Forms at Your Fingertips • TEC60824

Note to the teacher: At the beginning of each month, make a copy of this page. Program each section with information such as to-do lists, birthdays, special events, meetings, duties, and materials to collect. Then use the sheet to plan for the month.

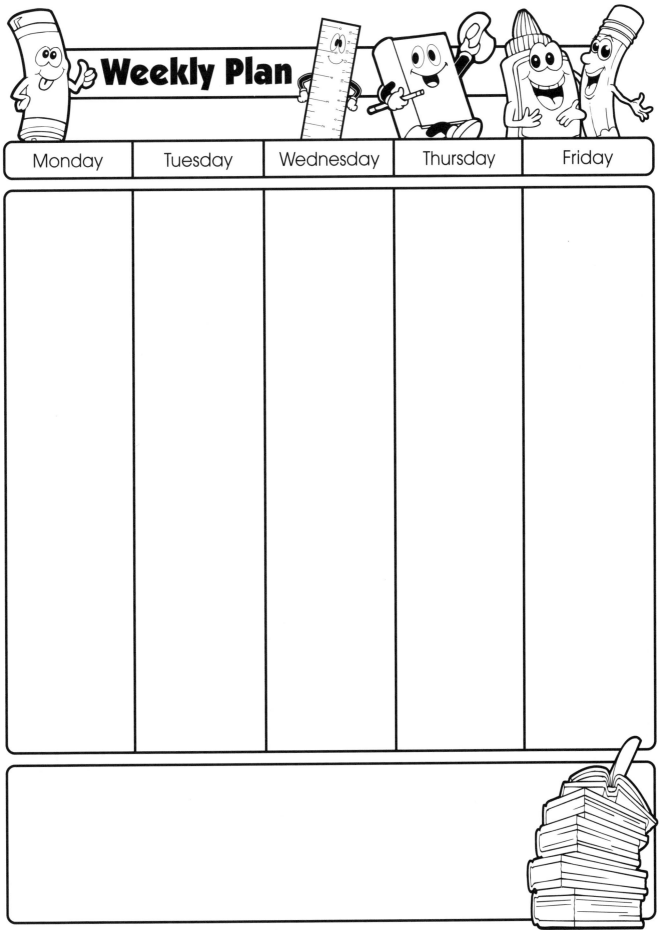

Weekly Plan

Monday	Tuesday	Wednesday	Thursday	Friday

©The Education Center, Inc. • *Forms at Your Fingertips* • TEC60824

SCHOOL INFORMATION

General Information

Teacher _____

Room Number _____

Principal _____

Assistant Principal _____

Secretary _____

Nurse _____

Guidance Counselor _____

Custodian _____

Grade-Level Teachers _____

Aide(s) _____

Special Teachers (name, day of week, time)

Music _____

Art _____

P. E. _____

Media Specialist _____

Resource _____

Other _____

Children With Special Needs

Health _____

Supervision _____

Learning _____

©The Education Center, Inc. • *Forms at Your Fingertips* • TEC60824

CLASSROOM PROCEDURES

Start of Day _____
_____
_____

Attendance _____
_____
_____

Fire Drill _____
_____

Recess _____
_____

Lunch/Milk Count _____
_____

Restroom Break _____
_____

Behavior Policy/Discipline _____
_____

Free Time _____
_____

End of Day _____
_____

Student Pull-Outs for Special Programs:

Name	Class	Day/Time

Helpful Students: _____
_____

Substitute Class Information Form

CLASS INFORMATION

_____ _____
teacher   date

Student Name	Bus No.	Parent's Name	Daytime Phone No.	Special Needs
1.				
2.				
3.				
4.				
5.				
6.				
7.				
8.				
9.				
10.				
11.				
12.				
13.				
14.				
15.				
16.				
17.				
18.				
19.				
20.				
21.				
22.				
23.				
24.				
25.				
26.				
27.				
28.				
29.				
30.				

©The Education Center, Inc. • Forms at Your Fingertips • TEC60824

SUBSTITUTE WEEKLY PLANS

Time	Monday	Tuesday	Wednesday	Thursday	Friday

Free-Time Activities _____

_____

_____

_____

Welcome to Room

©The Education Center, Inc. • Forms at Your Fingertips • TEC60824

EMERGENCY LESSON PLANS

Subject	Lesson

©The Education Center, Inc. • Forms at Your Fingertips • TEC60824

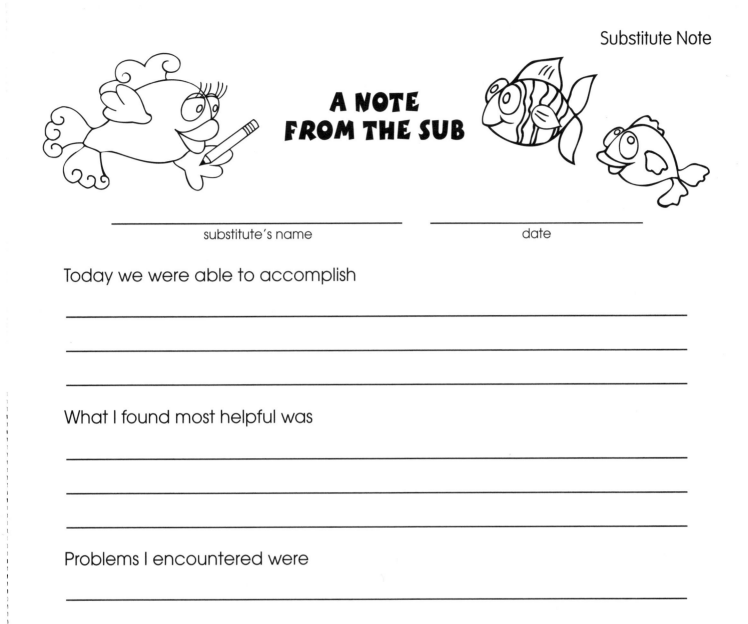

A NOTE FROM THE SUB

_____
substitute's name

_____
date

Today we were able to accomplish

_____

_____

_____

What I found most helpful was

_____

_____

_____

Problems I encountered were

_____

_____

_____

Additional comments

_____

_____

_____

Thank you for your help!

_____

©The Education Center, Inc. • Forms at Your Fingertips • TEC60824

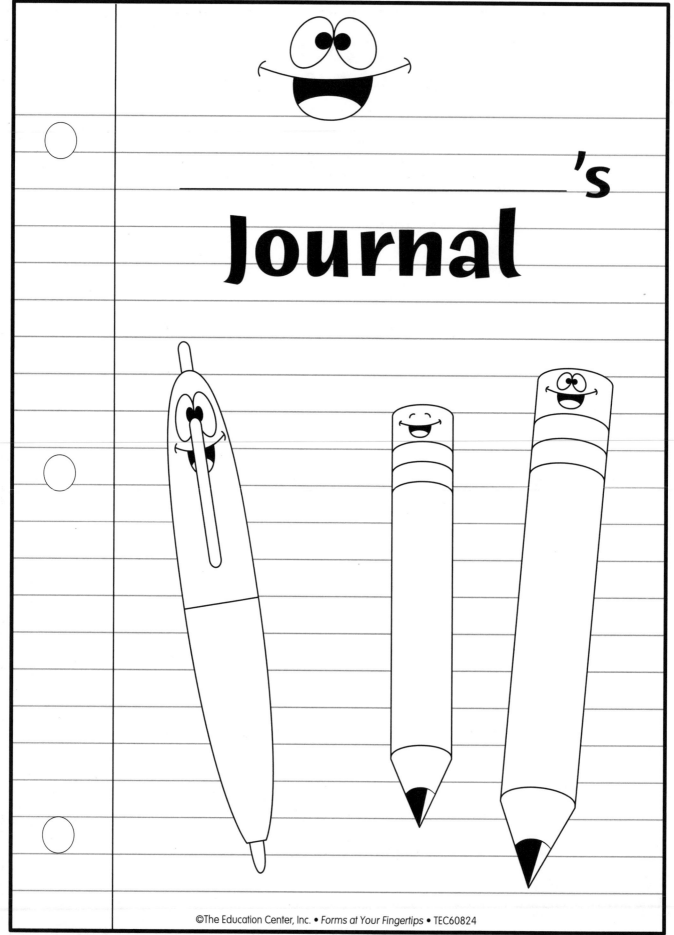

_____'s

Journal

©The Education Center, Inc. • *Forms at Your Fingertips* • TEC60824

Fall Journal

's

©The Education Center, Inc. • Forms at Your Fingertips • TEC60824

_____'s

WINTERTIME JOURNAL

©The Education Center, Inc. • Forms at Your Fingertips • TEC60824

_____ 's

Springtime Journal

©The Education Center, Inc. • Forms at Your Fingertips • TEC60824

's

Summertime Journal

©The Education Center, Inc. • Forms at Your Fingertips • TEC60824

Reading Contract

_____
date

I, _____, agree to read _____.
student   number of books or pages

To do this I will need to read _____ each day.
                               pages or minutes

I plan to complete this contract in _____.
                                    number of days or weeks

I will keep a record of my progress.

_____
student signature

_____
teacher signature

©The Education Center, Inc. • Forms at Your Fingertips • TEC60824

Reading Contract

_____
date

I, _____, agree to read _____.
student   number of books or pages

To do this I will need to read _____ each day.
                               pages or minutes

I plan to complete this contract in _____.
                                    number of days or weeks

I will keep a record of my progress.

_____
student signature

_____
teacher signature

©The Education Center, Inc. • Forms at Your Fingertips • TEC60824

Home Reading Record

Name _____

Date	Title (or type of material read)	Minutes	Pages	Parent Initials

©The Education Center, Inc. • Forms at Your Fingertips • TEC60824

Time for T. A. B. (Totally Awesome Books)!
Daily Reading Record

Name: _____ Date: _____

Title of book: _____

Starting page: _____ Ending page: _____

Parent's signature: _____

©The Education Center, Inc. • *Forms at Your Fingertips* • TEC60824

Time for T. A. B. (Totally Awesome Books)!
Daily Reading Record

Name: _____ Date: _____

Title of book: _____

Starting page: _____ Ending page: _____

Parent's signature: _____

©The Education Center, Inc. • *Forms at Your Fingertips* • TEC60824

Time for T. A. B. (Totally Awesome Books)!
Daily Reading Record

Name: _____ Date: _____

Title of book: _____

Starting page: _____ Ending page: _____

Parent's signature: _____

©The Education Center, Inc. • *Forms at Your Fingertips* • TEC60824

Time for T. A. B. (Totally Awesome Books)!
Daily Reading Record

Name: _____ Date: _____

Title of book: _____

Starting page: _____ Ending page: _____

Parent's signature: _____

©The Education Center, Inc. • *Forms at Your Fingertips* • TEC60824

Time for T. A. B. (Totally Awesome Books)!
Daily Reading Record

Name: _____ Date: _____

Title of book: _____

Starting page: _____ Ending page: _____

Parent's signature: _____

©The Education Center, Inc. • *Forms at Your Fingertips* • TEC60824

Book Recommendation Sheet

Name _____

If you like _____ books,

then _____

is for you because _____

_____

_____

_____

©The Education Center, Inc. • Forms at Your Fingertips • TEC60824

- -

Name _____

If you like _____ books,

then _____

is for you because _____

_____

_____

_____

©The Education Center, Inc. • Forms at Your Fingertips • TEC60824

Time to Talk
Would you like to be friends with the main character? Tell why or why not.

Time to Talk
Describe the story's setting. Can you easily picture it? Why or why not?

Time to Talk
What is the problem in the story? Tell how you think it might be solved.

Time to Talk
Talk about the most interesting thing that has happened in the story so far. What do you think will happen next?

Time to Talk
The theme of a story is a message the author wants to share about life. What do you think the author of your book is trying to say?

Time to Talk
If you could talk with the author, what questions would you ask?

Time to Talk
Compare this book to the last one you read. How is it the same? How is it different?

Time to Talk
Compare the main character with the main character in the last book you read. Would the two get along? Why or why not?

Time to Talk
Tell why this story seems realistic or unrealistic to you.

Time to Talk
Convince your partner to read your book by telling about its best parts.

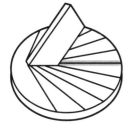

Time to Talk
In what genre does your book belong? Tell why it fits in that genre.

Time to Talk
If you could change one thing about your book, what would you change? Why?

©The Education Center, Inc. • *Forms at Your Fingertips* • TEC60824

Book Report Form

Name _____

Book Report

Title: _____

Author: _____

Type of book: _____ Number of pages: _____

Write a summary of the book.

_____

_____

_____

_____

_____

_____

What would you like to change about this book? _____

_____

_____

Write five interesting words from the book.
Use your dictionary to find the definition of each word.
Write the definitions on the lines.

1. _____

_____

2. _____

_____

3. _____

_____

4. _____

_____

5. _____

_____

©The Education Center, Inc. • Forms at Your Fingertips • TEC60824

VOCABULARY BOOKMARK

Name _____

Title & Author

Illustration

Word   Page   Meaning

1. _____   _____

2. _____   _____

3. _____   _____

4. _____   _____

5. _____   _____

6. _____   _____

7. _____   _____

8. _____   _____

9. _____   _____

10. _____   _____

Fold.

©The Education Center, Inc. • Forms at Your Fingertips • TEC60824

Note to the teacher: Give each student a copy of the bookmark. Before beginning reading, have the student cut out and personalize the bookmark, then fold it along the dashed line. Direct the student to use the bookmark to keep his page and to record ten new words and their meanings as he reads.

"PURR-FECTLY" SPECTACULAR SPELLING!

Use the chart below to help you study your spelling words. Put a check mark after you complete each step.

WORD LIST	1 Say the word.	2 Look at its parts.	3 Say the letters.	4 Close your eyes and spell the word.	5 Check your spelling.	6 Write the word.	7 Check your spelling.
1.							
2.							
3.							
4.							
5.							
6.							
7.							
8.							
9.							
10.							

©The Education Center, Inc. • Forms at Your Fingertips • TEC60824

Note to the teacher: At the beginning of each week, make one or more copies for each student to use in studying her spelling words.

Writing Assessment

Student's Name: _____ **Date:** _____

Title of Writing: _____

Assessment Items	Agree	Disagree
1. The writing selection has a topic sentence and concluding sentence.		
2. The purpose of the writing is clear (e.g. narrative, descriptive, explanatory, persuasive, etc.).		
3. The writing selection shows a logical order.		
4. The writing selection makes sense; it is easy to read.		
5. Specific details are used to enhance the explained steps.		
6. All details relate to the topic.		
7. Descriptive words and details are used.		
8. Transitional words such as *first, next, then,* and *finally* are used.		
9. Correct punctuation and capitalization are used.		
10. Each word is spelled correctly.		
11. Run-on sentences and incomplete sentences are avoided.		
12. Each verb agrees with its subject.		
13. All proper nouns are capitalized.		
14. Each paragraph is indented.		
15. Apostrophes are correctly used to form contractions and to show possession.		

Comments: _____

_____

_____

_____

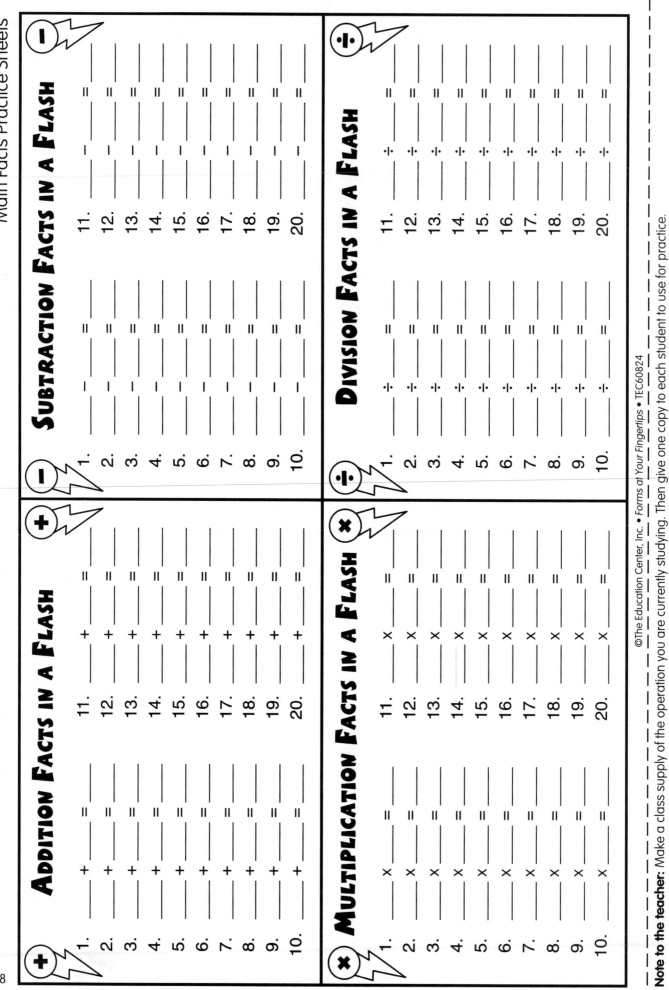

Addition Facts in a Flash

1. ___ + ___ = ___   11. ___ + ___ = ___
2. ___ + ___ = ___   12. ___ + ___ = ___
3. ___ + ___ = ___   13. ___ + ___ = ___
4. ___ + ___ = ___   14. ___ + ___ = ___
5. ___ + ___ = ___   15. ___ + ___ = ___
6. ___ + ___ = ___   16. ___ + ___ = ___
7. ___ + ___ = ___   17. ___ + ___ = ___
8. ___ + ___ = ___   18. ___ + ___ = ___
9. ___ + ___ = ___   19. ___ + ___ = ___
10. ___ + ___ = ___   20. ___ + ___ = ___

Subtraction Facts in a Flash

1. ___ − ___ = ___   11. ___ − ___ = ___
2. ___ − ___ = ___   12. ___ − ___ = ___
3. ___ − ___ = ___   13. ___ − ___ = ___
4. ___ − ___ = ___   14. ___ − ___ = ___
5. ___ − ___ = ___   15. ___ − ___ = ___
6. ___ − ___ = ___   16. ___ − ___ = ___
7. ___ − ___ = ___   17. ___ − ___ = ___
8. ___ − ___ = ___   18. ___ − ___ = ___
9. ___ − ___ = ___   19. ___ − ___ = ___
10. ___ − ___ = ___   20. ___ − ___ = ___

Multiplication Facts in a Flash

1. ___ × ___ = ___   11. ___ × ___ = ___
2. ___ × ___ = ___   12. ___ × ___ = ___
3. ___ × ___ = ___   13. ___ × ___ = ___
4. ___ × ___ = ___   14. ___ × ___ = ___
5. ___ × ___ = ___   15. ___ × ___ = ___
6. ___ × ___ = ___   16. ___ × ___ = ___
7. ___ × ___ = ___   17. ___ × ___ = ___
8. ___ × ___ = ___   18. ___ × ___ = ___
9. ___ × ___ = ___   19. ___ × ___ = ___
10. ___ × ___ = ___   20. ___ × ___ = ___

Division Facts in a Flash

1. ___ ÷ ___ = ___   11. ___ ÷ ___ = ___
2. ___ ÷ ___ = ___   12. ___ ÷ ___ = ___
3. ___ ÷ ___ = ___   13. ___ ÷ ___ = ___
4. ___ ÷ ___ = ___   14. ___ ÷ ___ = ___
5. ___ ÷ ___ = ___   15. ___ ÷ ___ = ___
6. ___ ÷ ___ = ___   16. ___ ÷ ___ = ___
7. ___ ÷ ___ = ___   17. ___ ÷ ___ = ___
8. ___ ÷ ___ = ___   18. ___ ÷ ___ = ___
9. ___ ÷ ___ = ___   19. ___ ÷ ___ = ___
10. ___ ÷ ___ = ___   20. ___ ÷ ___ = ___

©The Education Center, Inc. • Forms at Your Fingertips • TEC60824

Note to the teacher: Make a class supply of the operation you are currently studying. Then give one copy to each student to use for practice.

My Science Journal

_____
name

©The Education Center, Inc. • *Forms at Your Fingertips* • TEC60824

---

name _____ date _____

_____
science experience

① Briefly describe the experience: _____
_____
_____

② What special materials, if any, were used? _____
_____
_____

③ Write a sentence describing something new you learned. _____
_____

④ In the space below, draw a diagram or picture that would help you describe this science experience to a friend.

©The Education Center, Inc. • *Forms at Your Fingertips* • TEC60824

Note to the teacher: Give each student a copy of these forms. Have him color and personalize the journal cover and then complete the journaling page after a lab activity, class experiment, or field trip.

Research Report Rubric

Name: _____

Teacher's comments: _____

Topic: _____

Content and Details	Content is very informative and accurate. Report has many supporting details and is interesting to read.	Content is informative and mostly accurate. Report has adequate details.	Content is not always re-lated to the topic. Many in-accuracies. Few supporting details.	Content is not relevant or accurate. No details.
Organization	Report is well organized with a strong beginning, middle, and ending.	Report shows adequate organization. It has a begin-ning, middle, and ending.	Report is poorly organized and confusing at times.	Report has no organization.
Writing Mechanics and Readability	Report has few or no errors in spelling, punctuation, and/or grammar. Report is easy to read.	Report has a few to several errors in spelling, punc-tuation, and/or grammar. Report is readable.	Report has many errors in spelling, punctuation, and/or grammar. Report is difficult to read.	Report is unreadable.
Notecards	Notecards are completed and labeled correctly.	Most notecards are com-pleted and labeled correctly.	Some notecards are com-pleted and labeled correctly.	No notecards.
Bibliography	Bibliography is completed and written in correct form.	Bibliography is done but incomplete in parts. Some errors in form.	Bibliography is incomplete. Many errors in form.	No bibliography.
(Other)			

©The Education Center, Inc. • Forms at Your Fingertips • TEC60824

Note to the teacher: Make one copy for each student. Use the rubric for grading purposes. Or have the student use it to evaluate her own work, lightly shading each box that describes her report.

 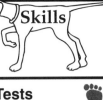

POINTERS FOR...

Completing Assignments

- Know exactly what your assignment is and when it is due.
- Decide how much time you'll need to do the assignment.
- Plan a time to do the assignment.
- Choose a quiet place to work.
- Gather all the books, paper, pencils, markers, and folders you'll need to do the assignment.
- Read the directions for the assignment carefully.
- Decide how much of the assignment you'll finish before taking a break.
- Do the assignment neatly; then check it for mistakes.

Managing Your Time

- Make a daily to-do list. Number the tasks from most to least important. Cross out each task as you complete it.
- Use a weekly planner or a calendar to mark when different assignments are due. Plan your work and play time around these due dates.
- Work on your toughest assignments during the time of day when you work best.
- Make a hard assignment, such as a research project, easier by breaking it down into smaller parts. Decide how much of the assignment you'll need to finish by certain days in order to meet the due date.

Taking Notes

- Listen carefully.
- Write down only the important words and phrases.
- Use abbreviations and symbols whenever you can.
- Show the importance of your notes by numbering them from most important to least important.

Taking Tests

Essay Tests
- Read the question twice to make sure you understand whether you are to *compare/contrast, define, describe, explain, list,* or *prove* your answer.
- Change the test question into the first sentence of your answer.
- Decide on the best order for the details of your answer.
- Write your answer as a paragraph. Reread your answer to make sure nothing was left out.

True/False Tests
- Read the whole question before answering it.
- Look for words—such as *all, every, always,* and *never*—that often make a statement false.
- To mark an answer true, all parts of it must be true. If only part of a statement is true, mark it false.

Matching Tests
- Read both lists before making any matches.
- Unless the directions say you can use an answer more than once, cross out each answer as you match it.

Multiple-Choice Tests
- Read the directions to find out if you're to look for the *correct* answer or the *best* answer.
- Read *all* the answer choices before deciding on your answer.
- Look for tricky words such as *not, never, except,* and *unless* that can change a question's meaning.

Fill-in-the-Blank Tests
- Count the number of blanks in each question to know how many words to write for an answer.
- Decide what word or number best answers that question and write it in the blank.

©The Education Center, Inc. • *Forms at Your Fingertips* • TEC60824

CHAPTER CHART

Study Point #1

Question/Answer

Study Point #2

Summarize

This simple chart can help you remember what you read. As you read an assignment, write a question for each page in the space below. Record the page number where the answer can be found. Then write the answer. When you've finished reading the entire assignment, write a few sentences telling what you learned in the summary space. What an easy way to study!

Page Read	Question	Answer	Page Number of Answer

Summary:

©The Education Center, Inc. • *Forms at Your Fingertips* • TEC60824

Note to the teacher: Give a copy of this chart to each student whenever he reads in his textbook. Have him keep his completed charts in a folder to use when studying for a unit test.

LOOK WHAT'S AHEAD!

Date _____

Dear Parent,

Learning how to be responsible is an important part of becoming a successful student. Organizing time wisely and planning ahead are skills every student needs.

Your child needs to start preparing for the following assignment:

PROJECT

Description: _____
_____
_____
Due date: _____
Additional comments: _____
_____
_____
_____
_____

TEST

Subject: _____
Date of test: _____
What to study: _____
_____
_____
_____
_____
_____
_____

Please encourage your child to work on this project or study for this test daily and not wait until the last minute. Then please sign below, cut on the dotted line, and have your child return the signed portion to school.

Thank you for assisting me in helping your child learn to be a responsible student.

Signed _____

- -

Cut on the dotted line and return the bottom portion only.

Student's Name _____

Parent's Signature _____

©The Education Center, Inc. • *Forms at Your Fingertips* • TEC60824

Note to the teacher: Before duplicating, complete the appropriate section; then date the letter and sign your name where indicated. Give each child a copy to take home at least one week before a major test and even earlier for a major project.

Name _____

Work Watcher

How did you do on _____?

Color a face to answer each question.

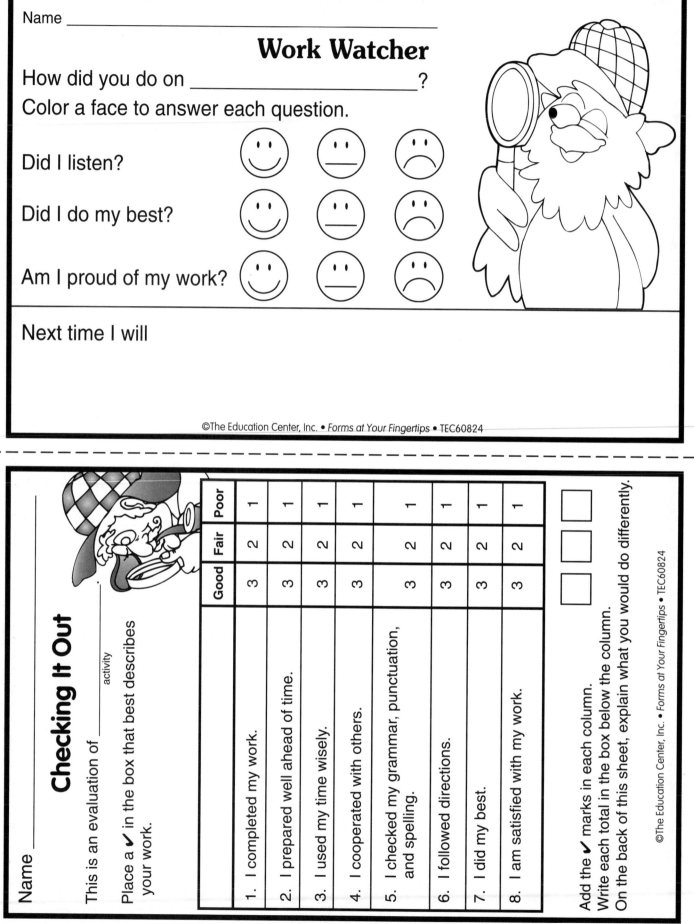

Did I listen?

Did I do my best?

Am I proud of my work?

Next time I will

©The Education Center, Inc. • *Forms at Your Fingertips* • TEC60824

Name _____

Checking It Out

This is an evaluation of _____.
activity

Place a ✔ in the box that best describes your work.

	Good	Fair	Poor
1. I completed my work.	3	2	1
2. I prepared well ahead of time.	3	2	1
3. I used my time wisely.	3	2	1
4. I cooperated with others.	3	2	1
5. I checked my grammar, punctuation, and spelling.	3	2	1
6. I followed directions.	3	2	1
7. I did my best.	3	2	1
8. I am satisfied with my work.	3	2	1

Add the ✔ marks in each column.
Write each total in the box below the column.
On the back of this sheet, explain what you would do differently.

☐ ☐ ☐

©The Education Center, Inc. • *Forms at Your Fingertips* • TEC60824

Center Tracking Sheet

Name: _____ Date: _____

1. Math		2. Language Arts	
3. Science		4. Social Studies	
5. Reading		6. Writing	
7.		8.	
9.		10.	

©The Education Center, Inc. • *Forms at Your Fingertips* • TEC60824

Note to teacher: Make one copy of this page and program any additional centers. Make copies for your students. Check off or stamp the marked squares as each child completes the centers.

Programmable Cards: Back-to-School

©The Education Center, Inc. • *Forms at Your Fingertips* • TEC60824

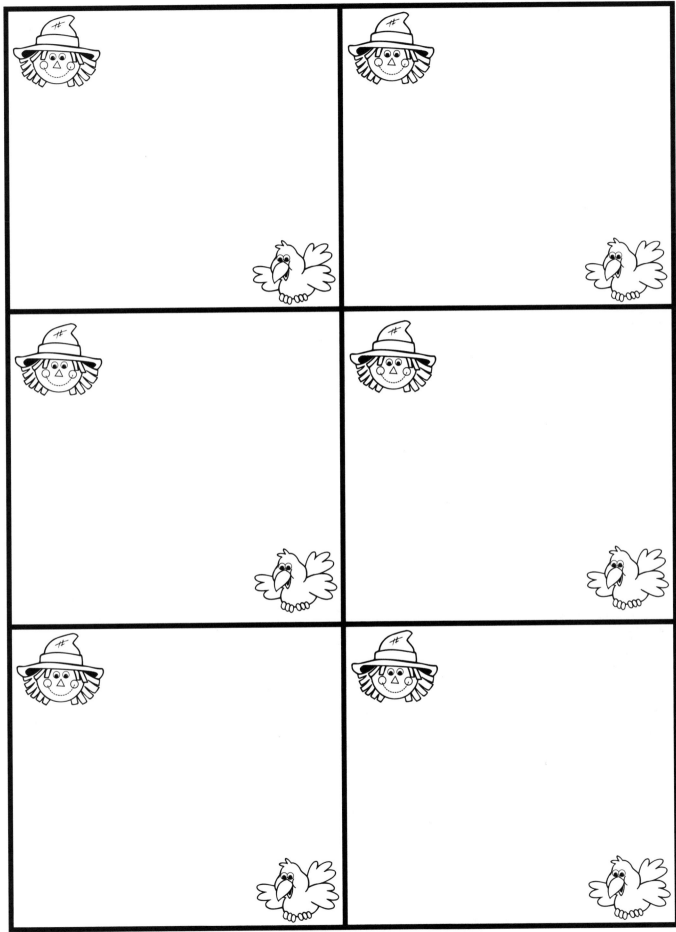

©The Education Center, Inc. • Forms at Your Fingertips • TEC60824

©The Education Center, Inc. • *Forms at Your Fingertips* • TEC60824

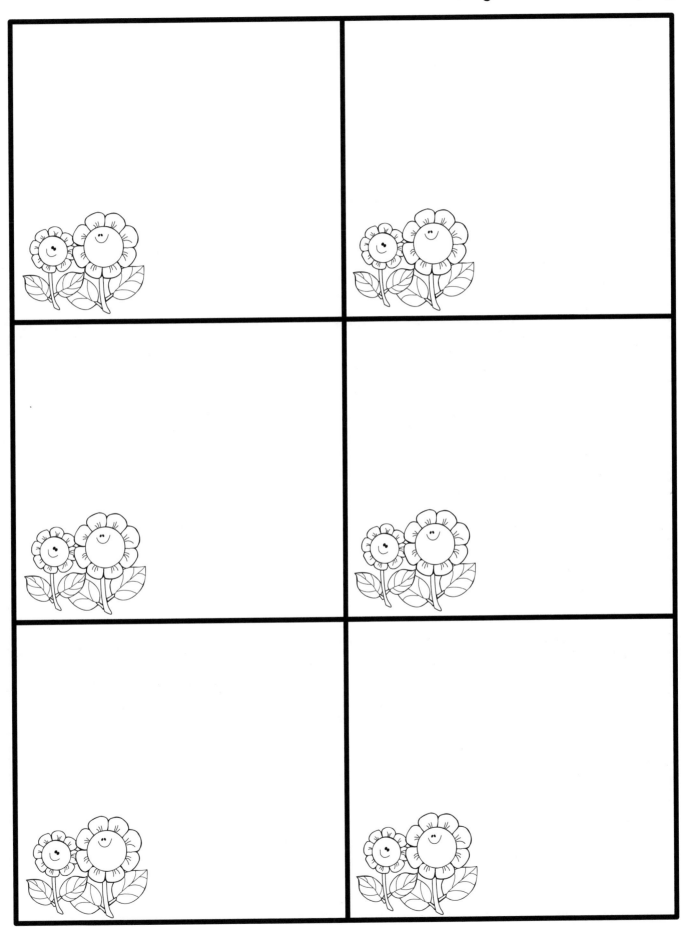

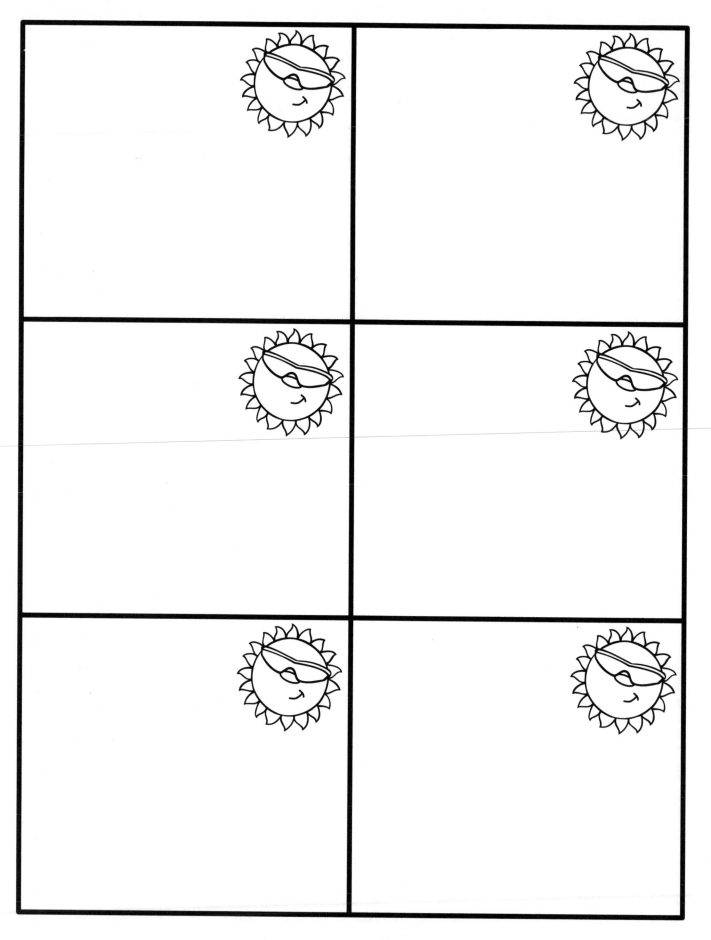

©The Education Center, Inc. • Forms at Your Fingertips • TEC60824

81

Dear _____,

　　Welcome to _____! I am excited about having you in my class.

　　Our school day begins at _____. This year we will be
learning about _____
time
_____
_____
_____

　　Here are some things you may bring to school:
_____
_____
_____

　　I am anxious to learn more about you and the things you enjoy.

Your teacher,

_____

©The Education Center, Inc. • Forms at Your Fingertips • TEC60824

You're invited to an open house!

Date: _____

Time: _____

Room: _____

Hope to see you there!

©The Education Center, Inc. • Forms at Your Fingertips • TEC60824

You're invited to an open house!

Date: _____

Time: _____

Room: _____

Hope to see you there!

©The Education Center, Inc. • Forms at Your Fingertips • TEC60824

You're invited to an open house!

Date: _____

Time: _____

Room: _____

Hope to see you there!

©The Education Center, Inc. • Forms at Your Fingertips • TEC60824

You're invited to an open house!

Date: _____

Time: _____

Room: _____

Hope to see you there!

©The Education Center, Inc. • Forms at Your Fingertips • TEC60824

Welcome to Open House!

Please sign in.

Your Name	Child's Name

©The Education Center, Inc. • Forms at Your Fingertips • TEC60824

Thank you for attending our open house. We appreciate your support!

Sincerely,

_____
teacher

©The Education Center, Inc. • *Forms at Your Fingertips* • TEC60824

Thank you for attending our open house. We appreciate your support!

Sincerely,

_____
teacher

©The Education Center, Inc. • *Forms at Your Fingertips* • TEC60824

Thank you for attending our open house. We appreciate your support!

Sincerely,

_____
teacher

©The Education Center, Inc. • *Forms at Your Fingertips* • TEC60824

Thank you for attending our open house. We appreciate your support!

Sincerely,

_____
teacher

©The Education Center, Inc. • *Forms at Your Fingertips* • TEC60824

Dear Parent,

Your conference for _____ has been scheduled at _____ on _____ , _____ .

Please complete the bottom portion of this form and return it to me as soon as possible.

I'm looking forward to visiting with you.

Sincerely,

_____
teacher

1   2   3   4   5

☐ I plan to attend my child's conference at the scheduled time.
☐ I will need to reschedule our conference.

_____   _____
child's name   parent signature

©The Education Center, Inc. • Forms at Your Fingertips • TEC60824

Dear Parent,

Your conference for _____ has been scheduled at _____ on _____ , _____ .

Please complete the bottom portion of this form and return it to me as soon as possible.

I'm looking forward to visiting with you.

Sincerely,

_____
teacher

1   2   3   4   5

☐ I plan to attend my child's conference at the scheduled time.
☐ I will need to reschedule our conference.

_____   _____
child's name   parent signature

©The Education Center, Inc. • Forms at Your Fingertips • TEC60824

Conference Questionnaire

	1	2	3	4	5	6

_____
date

Dear _____ ,

Would you please take a few minutes to answer the questions below? Your responses will help us prepare for our upcoming conference. I look forward to meeting with you on

_____ .

Please return this questionnaire before our scheduled conference day.

Thank you,

_____
teacher

- What subject(s) does your child enjoy most? _____
  Why? _____
  _____
  _____

- What subject(s) seems difficult for your child? _____
  Why? _____
  _____
  _____

- About how much time does your child spend each night with homework and reading?
  _____

- Does your child participate in any after-school activities? _____
  If so, please list them: _____
  _____

- Please list any concerns that you think we should address during our conference:
  _____
  _____
  _____

Parent-Teacher Conference Report

Date: _____
Student: _____
Grade: _____
Teacher: _____

SUBJECTS

	Progress				Effort			
	Excellent	Satisfactory	Needs Improvement	Unsatisfactory	Excellent	Satisfactory	Needs Improvement	Unsatisfactory
Reading								
Math								
Language								
Penmanship								
Spelling								
Science								
Social Studies								
Other:								

SPECIAL SUBJECTS

	Progress				Effort			
Art								
Music								
Library								
Computer								
P.E.								
Other:								

WORK HABITS

	Excellent	Satisfactory	Needs Improvement	Unsatisfactory
Listens				
Follows directions				
Works independently				
Works accurately				
Works neatly				
Completes work on time				

ATTITUDES

	Excellent	Satisfactory	Needs Improvement	Unsatisfactory
Gets along with others				
Is courteous and cooperates				
Demonstrates self-control				
Shows respect for others				
Cares for personal property				
Assumes responsibility for actions				

Days absent: _____ Days tardy: _____

Comments: _____

Teacher signature: _____

Parent signature: _____

©The Education Center, Inc. • Forms at Your Fingertips • TEC60824

Conference Schedule

_____
conference date

_____
teacher

7:30 _____

7:45 _____

8:00 _____

8:15 _____

8:30 _____

8:45 _____

9:00 _____

9:15 _____

9:30 _____

9:45 _____

10:00 _____

10:15 _____

10:30 _____

10:45 _____

11:00 _____

11:15 _____

11:30 _____

11:45 _____

12:00 _____

12:15 _____

12:30 _____

12:45 _____

1:00 _____

1:15 _____

1:30 _____

1:45 _____

2:00 _____

2:15 _____

2:30 _____

2:45 _____

3:00 _____

3:15 _____

3:30 _____

3:45 _____

4:00 _____

Additional Conferences

_____

_____

_____

_____

_____

_____

_____

_____

_____

_____

Thank you for coming
to your child's
parent-teacher conference.
Your attendance is
appreciated!

Sincerely,

_____
teacher

©The Education Center, Inc. • *Forms at Your Fingertips* • TEC60824

Thank you for coming
to your child's
parent-teacher conference.
Your attendance is
appreciated!

Sincerely,

_____
teacher

©The Education Center, Inc. • *Forms at Your Fingertips* • TEC60824

Thank you for coming
to your child's
parent-teacher conference.
Your attendance is
appreciated!

Sincerely,

_____
teacher

©The Education Center, Inc. • *Forms at Your Fingertips* • TEC60824

Thank you for coming
to your child's
parent-teacher conference.
Your attendance is
appreciated!

Sincerely,

_____
teacher

©The Education Center, Inc. • *Forms at Your Fingertips* • TEC60824

Classroom Times

Teacher: _____ Date: _____

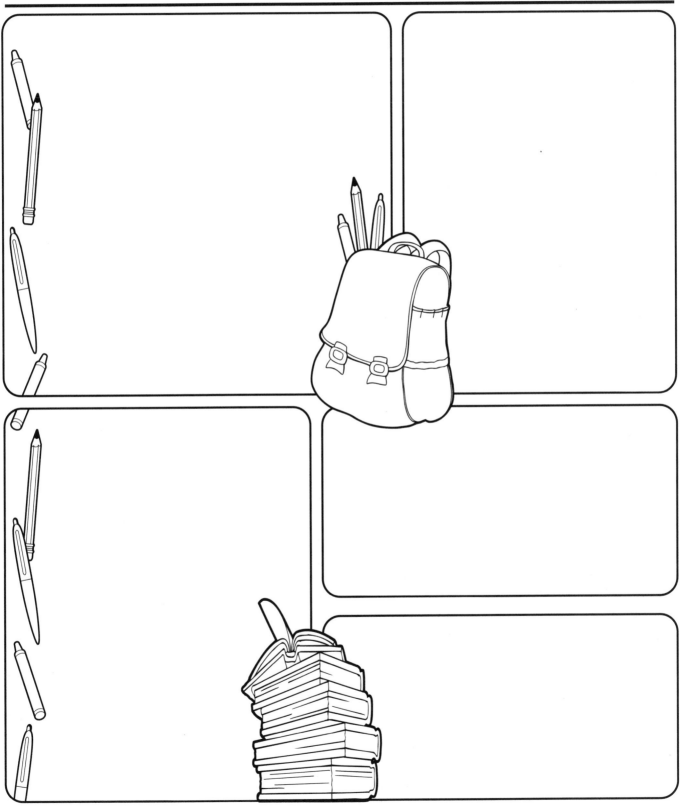

Classroom Times

Teacher: _____ Date: _____

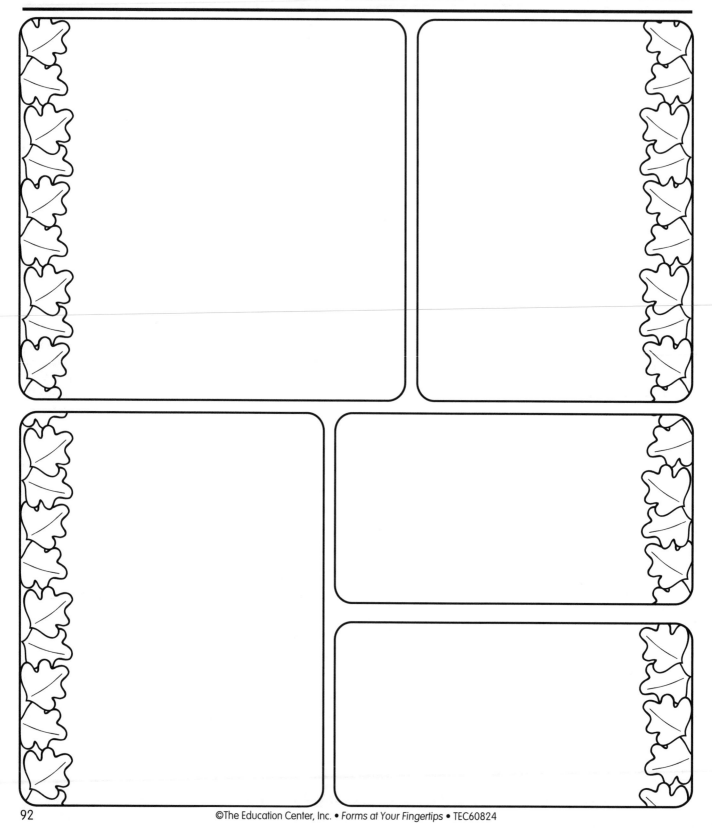

 ©The Education Center, Inc. • *Forms at Your Fingertips* • TEC60824

Classroom Times

Teacher: _____ Date: _____

Classroom Times

Teacher: _____   Date: _____

©The Education Center, Inc. • Forms at Your Fingertips • TEC60824

Classroom Times

Teacher: _____   Date: _____

School Note

©The Education Center, Inc. • *Forms at Your Fingertips* • TEC60824

SCHOOL NOTE

©The Education Center, Inc. • *Forms at Your Fingertips* • TEC60824

SCHOOL NOTE

©The Education Center, Inc. • Forms at Your Fingertips • TEC60824

School Note

©The Education Center, Inc. • Forms at Your Fingertips • TEC60824

School Note

©The Education Center, Inc. • *Forms at Your Fingertips* • TEC60824

School Note

©The Education Center, Inc. • *Forms at Your Fingertips* • TEC60824

SCHOOL NOTE

©The Education Center, Inc. • *Forms at Your Fingertips* • TEC60824

SCHOOL NOTE

©The Education Center, Inc. • *Forms at Your Fingertips* • TEC60824

School Note

©The Education Center, Inc. • *Forms at Your Fingertips* • TEC60824

SCHOOL NOTE

©The Education Center, Inc. • *Forms at Your Fingertips* • TEC60824

Missed Assignments

_____
date

Dear Parent,

_____ needs to complete the following assignments: _____

_____

_____

The work is due by _____ .

Your help and support are greatly appreciated.

Sincerely,

_____
teacher

Please sign and return.

_____
parent

ASSIGNMENT BOOK

©The Education Center, Inc. • Forms at Your Fingertips • TEC60824

Missed Assignments

_____
date

Dear Parent,

_____ needs to complete the following assignments: _____

_____

_____

The work is due by _____ .

Your help and support are greatly appreciated.

Sincerely,

_____
teacher

Please sign and return.

_____
parent

ASSIGNMENT BOOK

©The Education Center, Inc. • Forms at Your Fingertips • TEC60824

Extra Help Needed

Dear Parent,

_____ needs extra

help with _____ .

Here are some suggestions for how you can help

your child at home: _____

_____

_____

_____

Thank you!
Sincerely,

_____   _____
           teacher   date

©The Education Center, Inc. • Forms at Your Fingertips • TEC60824

Extra Help Needed

Dear Parent,

_____ needs extra

help with _____ .

Here are some suggestions for how you can help

your child at home: _____

_____

_____

_____

Thank you!
Sincerely,

_____   _____
           teacher   date

©The Education Center, Inc. • Forms at Your Fingertips • TEC60824

Name: _____   Date: _____

Weekly Progress Report

Work Habits
- [ ] Works independently and completes work
- [ ] Needs some assistance
- [ ] Needs a great deal of assistance
- [ ] Is easily distracted

Behavior
- [ ] Excellent
- [ ] Good
- [ ] Showing improvement
- [ ] Needs improvement

Effort/Attitude
- [ ] Excellent
- [ ] Average
- [ ] Good
- [ ] Needs improvement

Additional comments:
_____
_____
_____
_____

Sign and return the report to school. Your comments are always appreciated. If you need additional space, use the back of the report or another sheet of paper.

_____
parent's signature

©The Education Center, Inc. • *Forms at Your Fingertips* • TEC60824

Weekly Progress Report

name _____ date _____

Your child is showing progress by
- [ ] an improved attitude.
- [ ] improved effort.
- [ ] maintaining a passing grade average.
- [ ] an improved grade average.
- [ ] completing work.
- [ ] using time wisely.

Difficulties are attributed to
- [ ] frequent absences.
- [ ] poor work habits.
- [ ] low skill level in _____
- [ ] other _____

Suggestions:
_____
_____
_____
_____
_____

- [ ] If checked, please sign and return.

_____ teacher signature

_____ parent signature

©The Education Center, Inc. • *Forms at Your Fingertips* • TEC60824

Midterm Progress Report _____
date

Dear Parent,

This progress report is an informal evaluation of your child's progress for the first half of this grading period. Please discuss this report with your child.

The overall quality of _____'s work has been
- ☐ commendable.
- ☐ an improvement.
- ☐ below the regular performance.
- ☐ unsatisfactory in some areas.

Classwork has been
- ☐ excellent.
- ☐ satisfactory.
- ☐ unsatisfactory in

_____ .

Test performance has been
- ☐ excellent.
- ☐ satisfactory.
- ☐ unsatisfactory in

_____ .

A conference is ☐ not necessary. ☐ requested. Please call.

Teacher comment: _____
_____

_____
teacher signature

Parent comment: _____
_____

_____
parent signature

Please sign and return.

©The Education Center, Inc. • *Forms at Your Fingertips* • TEC60824

Money Due

Dear Parent,

_____ owes
<small>student</small>

_____ for _____.
<small>amount</small>   <small>reason</small>

Please return the money to school in this envelope by

_____.
<small>date</small>

Sincerely,

_____
<small>teacher</small>

©The Education Center, Inc. • Forms at Your Fingertips • TEC60824

Money Due

Dear Parent,

_____ owes
<small>student</small>

_____ for _____.
<small>amount</small>   <small>reason</small>

Please return the money to school in this envelope by

_____.
<small>date</small>

Sincerely,

_____
<small>teacher</small>

©The Education Center, Inc. • Forms at Your Fingertips • TEC60824

Money Due

Dear Parent,

_____ owes
<small>student</small>

_____ for _____.
<small>amount</small>   <small>reason</small>

Please return the money to school in this envelope by

_____.
<small>date</small>

Sincerely,

_____
<small>teacher</small>

©The Education Center, Inc. • Forms at Your Fingertips • TEC60824

REMINDER!

Library books
are due

_____ .
date

©The Education Center, Inc. • *Forms at Your Fingertips* • TEC60824

REMINDER!

Library books
are due

_____ .
date

©The Education Center, Inc. • *Forms at Your Fingertips* • TEC60824

REMINDER!

Library books
are due

_____ .
date

©The Education Center, Inc. • *Forms at Your Fingertips* • TEC60824

REMINDER!

Library books
are due

_____ .
date

©The Education Center, Inc. • *Forms at Your Fingertips* • TEC60824

School Supplies

Dear Parent,

_____ needs the following
school supplies:

©The Education Center, Inc. • Forms at Your Fingertips • TEC60824

School Supplies

Dear Parent,

_____ needs the following
school supplies:

©The Education Center, Inc. • Forms at Your Fingertips • TEC60824

Art Materials Request

Dear Parent,

Our class will be making lots of fun arts-and-crafts projects this year. We need your help to stock our art shelves. If possible, please send to school any of the items listed below. Thanks for your help!

Sincerely,

_____
teacher

©The Education Center, Inc. • Forms at Your Fingertips • TEC60824

Art Materials Request

Dear Parent,

Our class will be making lots of fun arts-and-crafts projects this year. We need your help to stock our art shelves. If possible, please send to school any of the items listed below. Thanks for your help!

Sincerely,

_____
teacher

©The Education Center, Inc. • Forms at Your Fingertips • TEC60824

Dear Family,

We need the following materials for a special class project:

_____

_____

_____

_____

_____

_____

If possible, please send in any of the items listed. Thanks for your support!

_____
teacher

©The Education Center, Inc. • *Forms at Your Fingertips* • TEC60824

Dear Family,

We need the following materials for a special class project:

_____

_____

_____

_____

_____

_____

If possible, please send in any of the items listed. Thanks for your support!

_____
teacher

©The Education Center, Inc. • *Forms at Your Fingertips* • TEC60824

Special Event Field Trip

Dear Parent,

Our class has the opportunity to visit _____

on _____ . This experience will enrich your

child's knowledge of _____ .

Your child will need to bring:

- field trip permission slip (below)

- _____

- _____

We will leave at _____ and return by _____ .

Keep this note and post it at home as a reminder. Thank you.

Sincerely,

_____
teacher

©The Education Center, Inc. • *Forms at Your Fingertips* • TEC60824

_____ has my permission to go on the field trip to _____
location

on _____ .
date

_____ _____
parent signature   date

Special Event Field Trip

Dear Parent,

Our class has the opportunity to visit _____

on _____ . This experience will enrich your

child's knowledge of _____ .

Your child will need to bring:

- field trip permission slip (below)

- _____

- _____

We will leave at _____ and return by _____ .

Keep this note and post it at home as a reminder. Thank you.

Sincerely,

_____
teacher

©The Education Center, Inc. • *Forms at Your Fingertips* • TEC60824

_____ has my permission to go on the field trip to _____
location

on _____ .
date

_____ _____
parent signature   date

Field Trip Crew

Student's Name	Bus	Parent's Name	Daytime Phone	Special Needs
1.				
2.				
3.				
4.				
5.				
6.				
7.				
8.				
9.				
10.				
11.				
12.				
13.				
14.				
15.				

Volunteer _____ **School Phone** _____

©The Education Center, Inc. • Forms at Your Fingertips • TEC60824

Field Trip Evaluation

Please take a few minutes to complete this form and return it to school with your child. Thank you!

I really enjoyed

_____

_____

_____

_____

I did not like

_____

_____

_____

_____

Suggestions:

_____

_____

_____

_____

Please rate each of the following from 1–5 (5 = highest):

_____ appropriateness of the trip

_____ travel time

_____ lunch

_____ interest/enjoyment

_____ other _____

©The Education Center, Inc. • Forms at Your Fingertips • TEC60824

Dear Parent,
We will be participating in the following activity which involves some time after school: _____

Your child is welcome to participate on _____ from _____
                                         date   time
to _____.
     time

Please complete the form below granting your permission. Return it to school with your child. Thank you.

_____
teacher

©The Education Center, Inc. • Forms at Your Fingertips • TEC60824

_____ has my
child

permission to stay after school on _____ from _____
                                   date   time
to _____.
     time

I have made arrangements to
☐ have my child picked up by

_____
person

☐

_____
parent signature

_____
date

Dear Parent,
We will be participating in the following activity which involves some time after school: _____

Your child is welcome to participate on _____ from _____
                                         date   time
to _____.
     time

Please complete the form below granting your permission. Return it to school with your child. Thank you.

_____
teacher

©The Education Center, Inc. • Forms at Your Fingertips • TEC60824

_____ has my
child

permission to stay after school on _____ from _____
                                   date   time
to _____.
     time

I have made arrangements to
☐ have my child picked up by

_____
person

☐

_____
parent signature

_____
date

Parent Volunteer Information

Dear Parent,

It is helpful for me to gather information about my students' parents for upcoming projects and events. I value your interests and expertise, and I encourage you to share your talents with us. Please complete the form below and return it to school as soon as possible. Thanks!

Sincerely,

_____
teacher signature

Parent _____ Child _____

Address _____ Phone _____

I enjoy the following hobbies: _____

My profession is _____

I can contribute by

☐ being a parent helper ☐ making phone calls ☐ going on field trips
☐ supplying materials ☐ making projects at home ☐ other _____

Comments: _____
_____

©The Education Center, Inc. • *Forms at Your Fingertips* • TEC60824

Parent Volunteer Information

Dear Parent,

It is helpful for me to gather information about my students' parents for upcoming projects and events. I value your interests and expertise, and I encourage you to share your talents with us. Please complete the form below and return it to school as soon as possible. Thanks!

Sincerely,

_____
teacher signature

Parent _____ Child _____

Address _____ Phone _____

I enjoy the following hobbies: _____

My profession is _____

I can contribute by

☐ being a parent helper ☐ making phone calls ☐ going on field trips
☐ supplying materials ☐ making projects at home ☐ other _____

Comments: _____
_____

©The Education Center, Inc. • *Forms at Your Fingertips* • TEC60824

Injury Report

Dear Parent,

This is to report that _____ was injured at school.
name

Injury: _____

Treatment: _____

Treated by: _____

Follow-up suggestions: _____

_____

Please sign and return this notice. Thank you.

_____
teacher signature

_____   _____
parent signature   date

©The Education Center, Inc. • *Forms at Your Fingertips* • TEC60824

Injury Report

Dear Parent,

This is to report that _____ was injured at school.
name

Injury: _____

Treatment: _____

Treated by: _____

Follow-up suggestions: _____

_____

Please sign and return this notice. Thank you.

_____
teacher signature

_____   _____
parent signature   date

©The Education Center, Inc. • *Forms at Your Fingertips* • TEC60824

We're Celebrating!

Dear Parent,

We are celebrating _____

_____

at _____ on _____ ,
　　　　time　　　　　　　　　　　day

_____ . Please help us
　　　　　　date

celebrate by _____

_____

_____

_____

Thank you!　　　　　　Sincerely,

　　　　　　　　　　_____
　　　　　　　　　　　　　　　teacher

©The Education Center, Inc. • *Forms at Your Fingertips* • TEC60824

We're Celebrating!

Dear Parent,

We are celebrating _____

_____

at _____ on _____ ,
　　　　time　　　　　　　　　　　day

_____ . Please help us
　　　　　　date

celebrate by _____

_____

_____

_____

Thank you!　　　　　　Sincerely,

　　　　　　　　　　_____
　　　　　　　　　　　　　　　teacher

©The Education Center, Inc. • *Forms at Your Fingertips* • TEC60824

Halloween Party!

Dear Parent,

Our Halloween party will be at _____ ,
on _____
day

We will
time

celebrate by _____
date

_____ .

If you would like to help, please
check one of the boxes below and
return this note to school.

☐ I will provide snacks.
☐ I will help in the classroom.
☐ other _____

Sincerely,

_____
teacher

_____
parent signature

©The Education Center, Inc. • Forms at Your Fingertips • TEC60824

Thanksgiving Party

Dear Parent,

Our Thanksgiving party will be at _____
time

on _____ , _____ .
day   date

We will celebrate by _____

_____ .

If you would like to help, please check one of the
boxes below and return this note to school.

☐ I will provide snacks. _____
☐ I will help in the classroom.
☐ other _____

Sincerely,

_____   _____
parent signature   teacher signature

©The Education Center, Inc. • Forms at Your Fingertips • TEC60824

HOLIDAY CELEBRATION

Dear Parent,

Our holiday party will be at _____ on _____, _____ time . We will
date   day

celebrate by _____ .

If you would like to help, please check one of the boxes below and return this note to school. I will contact you with specifics in a few days.

☐ I can provide snacks.
☐ I can help in the classroom.
☐ other _____

Sincerely,

_____
teacher

_____
parent

©The Education Center, Inc. • Forms at Your Fingertips • TEC60824

HOLIDAY Party

Dear Parent,

Our holiday party will be at _____ time

on _____, _____ . We will celebrate by _____ .
day   date

If you would like to help, please check one of the boxes below and return this note to school.

☐ I will provide snacks.
☐ I will help in the classroom.
☐ other _____

Sincerely,

_____
teacher

_____
parent signature

©The Education Center, Inc. • Forms at Your Fingertips • TEC60824

Dear Parent,

VALENTINE'S DAY PARTY

Our valentine party will be at _____ on _____ ,
time   day
_____. We will celebrate by _____
date
_____.

If you would like to help, please check one of the boxes below and return this note to school.

☐ I will provide snacks.
☐ I will help in the classroom.
☐ other _____

Sincerely,

_____
teacher

_____
parent's signature

©The Education Center, Inc. • *Forms at Your Fingertips* • TEC60824

St. Patrick's Day Celebration

Dear Parent,

Our St. Patrick's Day celebration will be at _____ on
time
_____ , _____. We will celebrate by
day   date
_____.

If you would like to help, please check one of the boxes below and return this note to school.

☐ I will provide snacks.   ☐ I will help in the classroom.
☐ other _____

Sincerely,

_____
teacher

_____
parent signature

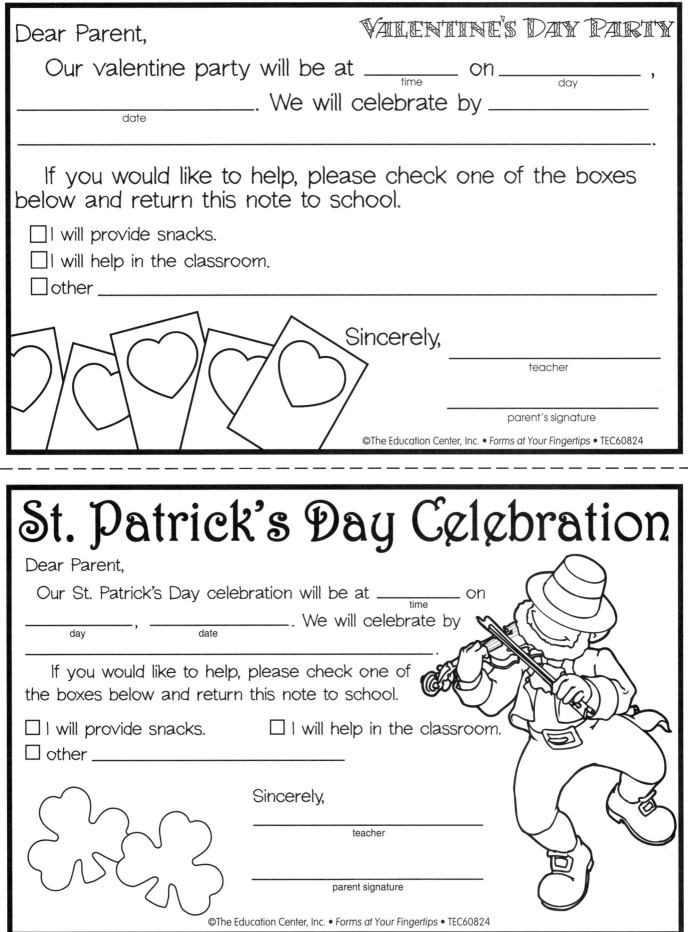

©The Education Center, Inc. • *Forms at Your Fingertips* • TEC60824

Our Valentine's Class List

Boys

Girls

Teachers:

©The Education Center, Inc. • *Forms at Your Fingertips* • TEC60824

Let's Celebrate!

Dear Parent,

Our end-of-the-year celebration will be at

_____ on _____ ,
time   day

_____ .
date

We will celebrate by _____

_____ .

If you would like to help, please check one of the boxes below and return this note to school.

☐ I will provide snacks.

☐ I will help in the classroom.

☐ other _____

_____
parent signature

Sincerely,

_____
teacher signature

©The Education Center, Inc. • Forms at Your Fingertips • TEC60824

Let's Celebrate!

Dear Parent,

Our end-of-the-year celebration will be at

_____ on _____ ,
time   day

_____ .
date

We will celebrate by _____

_____ .

If you would like to help, please check one of the boxes below and return this note to school.

☐ I will provide snacks.

☐ I will help in the classroom.

☐ other _____

_____
parent signature

Sincerely,

_____
teacher signature

©The Education Center, Inc. • Forms at Your Fingertips • TEC60824

Happy Halloween!

_____
name

_____
teacher

_____
date

©The Education Center, Inc. • Forms at Your Fingertips • TEC60824

_____
name

Gobbling to say...

Have a happy holiday!

_____
teacher

_____
date

©The Education Center, Inc. • Forms at Your Fingertips • TEC60824

Happy Holidays!

From Your Teacher

name

©The Education Center, Inc. • *Forms at Your Fingertips* • TEC60824

HAPPY NEW YEAR!

name

teacher

©The Education Center, Inc. • *Forms at Your Fingertips* • TEC60824

You're Just Dandy! Happy Valentine's Day!

_____
teacher

_____
date

©The Education Center, Inc. • Forms at Your Fingertips • TEC60824

_____
name

May the luck of the Irish be with you. Happy St. Patrick's Day!

_____
teacher

_____
date

©The Education Center, Inc. • Forms at Your Fingertips • TEC60824

Happy Birthday,

Here is my birthday wish for you:

From

©The Education Center, Inc. • Forms at Your Fingertips • TEC60824

Happy Birthday,

Here is my birthday wish for you:

From

©The Education Center, Inc. • Forms at Your Fingertips • TEC60824

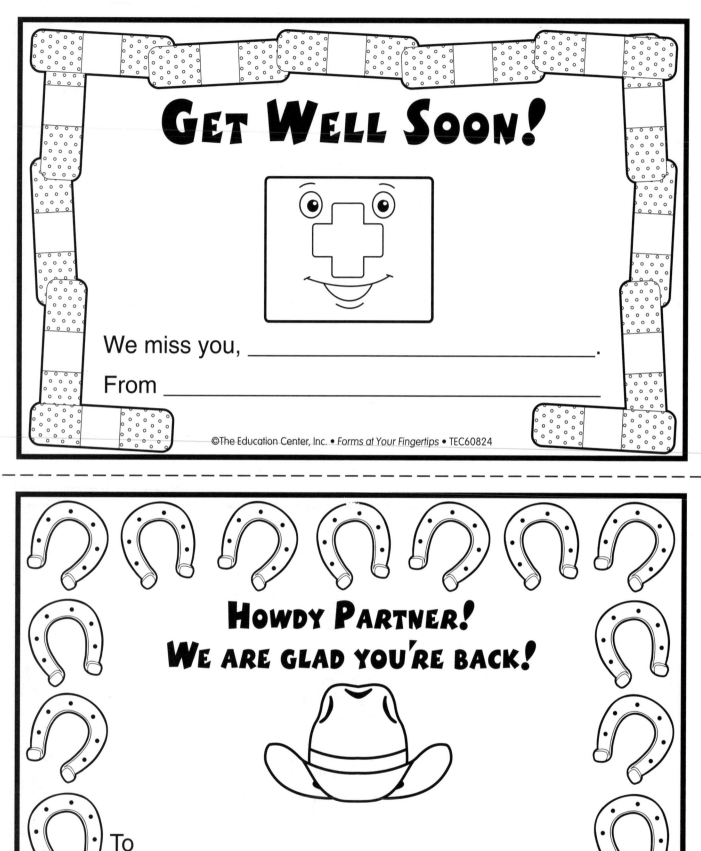

GET WELL SOON!

We miss you, _____.

From _____

©The Education Center, Inc. • Forms at Your Fingertips • TEC60824

HOWDY PARTNER!
WE ARE GLAD YOU'RE BACK!

To _____

From _____

©The Education Center, Inc. • Forms at Your Fingertips • TEC60824

_____
name

Thank you for your help with the

_____.

I really appreciate it!

From _____

©The Education Center, Inc. • *Forms at Your Fingertips* • TEC60824

You're Sweet,

_____.
name

Thank you for the gift!

©The Education Center, Inc. • *Forms at Your Fingertips* • TEC60824

Thank you!

Dear _____,

parent

Thank you for your help

with the _____.

We really appreciate it!

_____

teacher

©The Education Center, Inc. • Forms at Your Fingertips • TEC60824

Thank you!

Dear _____,

parent

Thank you for your help

with the _____.

We really appreciate it!

_____

teacher

©The Education Center, Inc. • Forms at Your Fingertips • TEC60824

Have You Heard?

_____
name

had a great day today!

_____   _____
date   teacher

©The Education Center, Inc. • *Forms at Your Fingertips* • TEC60824

_____
name

HAS BRUSHED UP ON

_____.

CONGRATULATIONS ON A JOB WELL DONE!

©The Education Center, Inc. • *Forms at Your Fingertips* • TEC60824

_____
name

YOU'RE ON THE RIGHT TRACK!

Keep up the good work in

_____ .

_____
teacher

_____
date

©The Education Center, Inc. • *Forms at Your Fingertips* • TEC60824

_____
name

THANKS FOR GOING THE EXTRA YARD!

_____
teacher

_____
date

©The Education Center, Inc. • *Forms at Your Fingertips* • TEC60824

_____
name

YOU'RE ONE SMART COOKIE!

_____
teacher

_____
date

©The Education Center, Inc. • _Forms at Your Fingertips_ • TEC60824

_____
name

Your attitude couldn't be "butter"!

Keep up the great work!

POPCORN

_____
teacher

©The Education Center, Inc. • _Forms at Your Fingertips_ • TEC60824

_____
name

Your attitude couldn't be "butter"!

Keep up the great work!

POPCORN

_____
teacher

©The Education Center, Inc. • _Forms at Your Fingertips_ • TEC60824

does "boo-tiful" work!

name

teacher

date

©The Education Center, Inc. • Forms at Your Fingertips • TEC60824

Gobblin' Good Work!

name

teacher

date

©The Education Center, Inc. • Forms at Your Fingertips • TEC60824

"Snow-body" Does It Better Than You!

Presented to

_____

for

_____

_____

_____   _____
teacher   date

©The Education Center, Inc. • Forms at Your Fingertips • TEC60824

"Snow" Foolin'!

_____
name

has
cool behavior!

_____
teacher

_____
date

©The Education Center, Inc. • Forms at Your Fingertips • TEC60824

Buzzing by to say

———————————————
name

had a super day!

You did a "bee-utiful" job on

———————————————

———————————————

———————————————.

———————————————
teacher

———————————————
date

©The Education Center, Inc. • Forms at Your Fingertips • TEC60824

———————————————'s
name

work is in full bloom!
Good job.

———————————————
teacher

———————————————
date

©The Education Center, Inc. • Forms at Your Fingertips • TEC60824

_____

name

had a "fin-tastic" day!

_____

teacher

_____

date

©The Education Center, Inc. • *Forms at Your Fingertips* • TEC60824

_____

name

WAS SPOTTED

_____

_____ •

WAY TO GO!

_____

teacher

_____

date

©The Education Center, Inc. • *Forms at Your Fingertips* • TEC60824

READING
Award

This award is given to

_____

for

_____

Presented the _____ day

of _____

Signed _____

©The Education Center, Inc. • Forms at Your Fingertips • TEC60824

Writing Award

This award is given to

_____

for

_____

Presented the _____

of _____ day

Signed _____

©The Education Center, Inc. • Forms at Your Fingertips • TEC60824

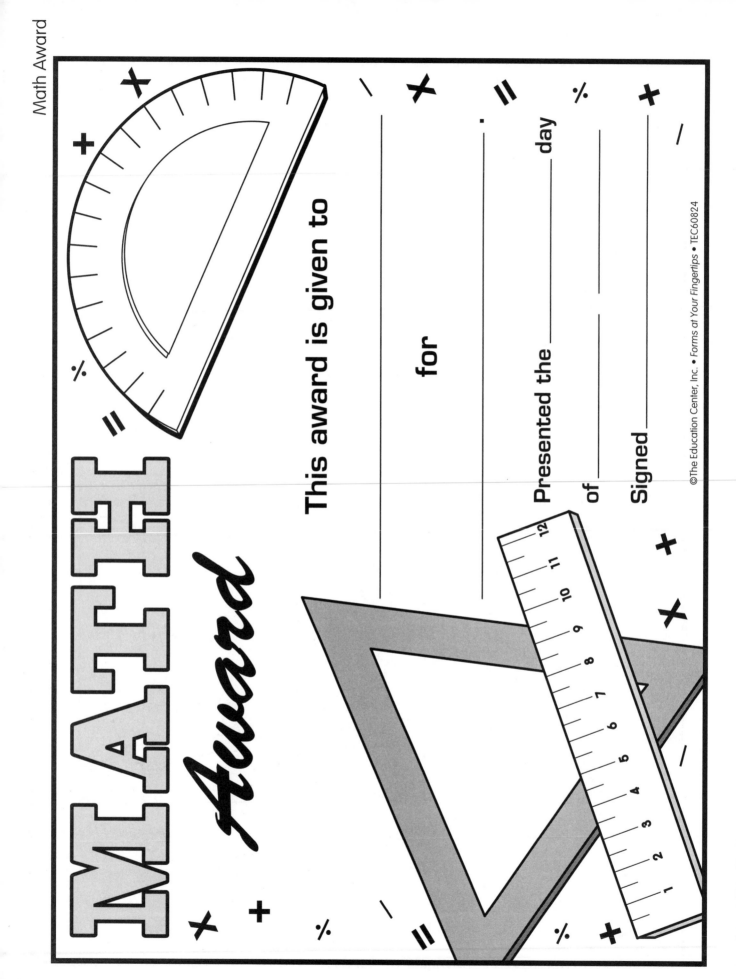

MATH Award

This award is given to

_____

for

_____

Presented the _____ day

of _____

Signed _____

©The Education Center, Inc. • Forms at Your Fingertips • TEC60824

SCIENCE AWARD

This award is given to

_____

for

_____

_____

Presented the _____ day

of _____

Signed _____

©The Education Center, Inc. • Forms at Your Fingertips • TEC60824

SOCIAL STUDIES

Award

This award is given to

_____

_____

for _____ .

Presented the _____ day

of _____

Signed _____

©The Education Center, Inc. • Forms at Your Fingertips • TEC60824

ACHIEVEMENT

Given to

this _____ day of _____

20 _____

Signed _____

©The Education Center, Inc. • Forms at Your Fingertips • TEC60824

_____
(name of adult)

is presented the

GOOD EGG AWARD
for "egg-cellent" character.

You have exhibited the following admirable traits:

1. _____

2. _____

3. _____

Congratulations!
We admire you!

_____
(name of class)

©The Education Center, Inc. • *Forms at Your Fingertips* • TEC60824

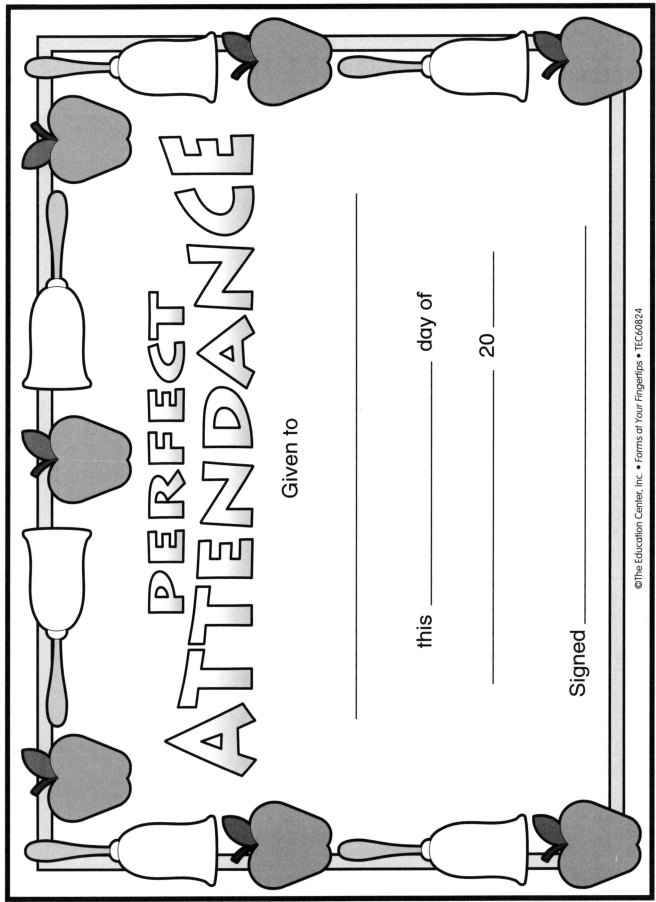

PERFECT ATTENDANCE

Given to

_____

this _____ day of

_____ 20 _____

Signed _____

©The Education Center, Inc. • Forms at Your Fingertips • TEC60824

HONOR ROLL

Given to

_____

this _____ day of _____

_____ 20 ____

Signed _____

EXCELLENT

©The Education Center, Inc. • Forms at Your Fingertips • TEC60824